WINDOW OF THE DARK WORLD

Josiah C. Racer

Trafford
PUBLISHING®

Trafford PUBLISHING®   www.trafford.com

North America & international
toll-free: 1 888 232 4444 (USA & Canada)
phone: 250 383 6864 ♦ fax: 250 383 6804 ♦ email: info@trafford.com

The United Kingdom & Europe
phone: +44 (0)1865 487 395 ♦ local rate: 0845 230 9601
facsimile: +44 (0)1865 481 507 ♦ email: info.uk@trafford.com

TABLE OF CONTENTS

DEDICATION

My beloved Parents; Mr. and Mrs. D.I Josiah and My beloved
Siblings. Also to Michael Ben, Yang Mei, Obi Prince and the all
the lovers of Christ.

Acknowledgement

This book is dedicated to my beloved parents, Mr. and Mrs. D.I Josiah, who instilled the fear of God in me and to my siblings, Godwin, Deborah, Emma, Josiah, Ezekiel and Eliza.

My special thanks to Yang Mei, for her love and concern toward the accomplishment of this work. Also to Rev. Basil and his wife, to Della, and Saint Jerry for their moral and spiritual supports. My Big brother and bosom friend, Michael Ben is very much appreciated for being like a father to me and for supporting all my endeavors. Thanks also to the rest of Michael's family. Lastly, my greatest gratitude to God Almighty, whose mercy and love endures forever. I pray that lives will be changed through this great whack on the ears of Christians.

INTRODUCTION

Every rank and file of Christ's disciples is inevitably involved in this titanic life struggle that follows our Christian race. It is not over until it is over. No warrior will compromise with his enemy not even in the battlefield, a good fighter cannot neglect the enemies' strength and weakness, for knowing how equipped your enemies are, will be your first step to victory. However, why do we cast out demons and embrace devil at the same time, rebuking Satan while we are comfortably enjoying his meal is the greatest mistake of our time.

Obviously, we have forgotten that his food nourishes nothing but shame, guilt, destruction and death. Slaves that love their chain can never be free. Therefore, anyone that craves for peace, spiritual prosperity and progress must not entangle himself with things that defiles.

This is the sole mystery revealed in this book; it will enlighten and direct you into a fulfilled spiritual alacrity and maturity. It is a poignant and awe-inspiring exposure of how Satan has taken hostage the lives of many. Also it revealed in-depth activities of Satan, remedies for addictions and a broad highlight on the rising acceptance of evil in our societies today.

In this book, you will be able to recognize and combat the enemies of Christ, recognize most tricks of Satan and understand the importance of making the "WORD" so strong in you that the enemies will not be able to pull you down. **This is a whack on the ears of Christians**.

Our Failures

*Ignorance of your enemy's strength and
weaknesses could spell defeat.*

The incessant consequential cataclysms in this horrendous evil world have different causes explored by various schools of thought. The manifestations thereof have been compiled, thus it calls for a careful examination, consideration and correction, for it is the rock on which this world and lives therein will wreck.

Just as the twentieth century draws to an end, a new millennium emerges on the horizon; everyone across this globe is confused and scared. We all are searching for true reality, desperate for a place of safety in a world beleaguered with sicknesses, war, terrorism, rampant crime, racial unrest, the threat of nuclear and biological warfare, environmental threats, pollution and lots more. The main reason for the miseries that outweigh so many hearts and lives today is as a consequence of the growing acceptance of evil in our ways of life which we have resolutely refused to acknowledge.

While we yearn for peace, we simply have forgotten that peace can never reign in any grubby and delusive mind; it can never be in a crooked generation that has deliberately neglected the norms of moral uprightness. It can never be in heart where the love for money and hustling for wealth has silenced the inner still small voice of man.

Not even in this generation where evil seems to be legislated, accustomed, denied, concealed, redefined and rationalized. It is much like entering into a darkened room and our eyes are gradually adjusting to the environment. Before long, bits and pieces that seemed too suspicious to handle soon became permissible to lay hold of. We became accustomed with darkness overnight, gone back to chase the dogs off our vomit.

Things that once were swept under the rug are now flaunted as freedoms that are guaranteed under the Constitution, --things like abortion, neo-Nazis on high school campuses, homosexual rights, New Age environmentalism and condom distribution.

Evil is redefined, drunkenness becomes alcoholism, adultery and fornication is merely an affair, sodomy is gay, pornography is adult literature, sex mate as boy/girlfriend and divorce as separation. Evil is real, and it is very important to call it by its name. Today's society promotes, encourages, and teaches young people to explore their sexuality and to become active in early adolescence. The media and advertisement firms are using the exploitation of the body more unashamedly than ever before.

Intimate physical details are no longer being airbrushed out of photographed models; such details are even being drawn on our national dailies and newsprint just for attraction and seduction. The Youths have been bombarded with assorted immoral spur by the media but parents, teachers, the clergy and even religious circles have remain silent on this subject, giving us up to self morals and destruction.

To convince the gullible, nearly everything from cosmetics to religion is presented as seeming different from what it really is; half truths, prejudices, slanted reporting, denigration, detraction, mythical argument, distortion of facts, falsifications, pretense of virtue while supporting vice and glorification of violence.

In our politics, impossible promises are made to honor, in our education destructive theories are formulated, in medicine false arguments will prevent the next generation from arriving on the earth, commerce falsifies advertisement on television, the press distorts the truth to suit a particular sect, the porno and the amoral people sell their stuff with the argument that somehow what is adult is sinless, that what may be bad for children is not bad for adults. Evil is concealed.

A student throws garbage on the classroom floor and defends his act on the ground that if the janitor did not have work to do, he would have no job, hence no income with which to support his family! Just like King Saul of Israel disobeyed Jehovah and refused to destroy the livestock booty taken from the Amalekites. He excused himself on this basis...the people spared the best of the sheep and oxen, to sacrifice unto Jehovah our God (1 Samuel 15:15).

Ever since Roe vs. Wade became law in 1973, more than 70 million innocent lives have been snuffed out. We abort our babies and defend the atrocity on the basis that we must not produce millions of youngsters who will not have adequate medical and educational facilities. Now we assumed, any unwanted pregnancy could be ended legally simply because a man-made law lifts the penalty of killing the innocent but it does not change God's legislation on the matter (Exodus 21:22-25).

Up till now we are shocked when we read about the human sacrifices of ancient times, we criticized ancient culture and customs while our unborn babies are regularly sacrificed on the altars of feminist ideology and convenience. We are stunned by the horrors of the German holocaust where nearly six million Jews lost their lives, yet over ten times that number of innocent babies has been killed.

We strive for the extinction of terrorism while we are the vilest terror to innocent babies. We seek peace and unity but we cannot reconcile with our unborn regeneration. Even the abortionists have engaged in the evil trade of selling baby parts for research to pharmaceutical companies, universities and research institutes.

This evil trade is probably the reason for initiating partial birth abortion procedure. The normal abortion procedures destroy the baby's body, so the abortionist devised ways of terminating pregnancy without damaging the body parts of the baby because they want to market the parts instead of wasting the entire body. In their dark conscience, they can make almost $2000 per baby depending on the parts ordered. What a dark world, yet we all yearn for change!

Think of it, can a society that kills off its own offspring just for convenience sake really continue to maintain a pervasively loving, peaceful and nurturing spirit toward its children in general? I think not! The temperament that calls for abortion on demand cannot annul itself from the source of evil that plagues our societies today. This is really ugly, killing your own son or daughter to solve your problem is even worst than the proclaimed ancient ritualism.

Ask yourself, what if you were aborted, what if you were removed from womb the very moment your conception was noticed. Your mother was very gracious and unselfish; she did not condemn you to death rather provided all necessary nutrients for your healthy growth and development but now we have the impudence to sit and execute capital judgment on the innocent for the sake of pleasure seeking and egotistical reasons.

Truly I say unto you, be it pregnancy resulting from rape or incest or that you are emotionally unprepared to enter parenthood, call it a casual sexual relationship with no prospect of marriage, diagnosis of abnormalities that may result to problems after birth or call it an abortion to survive pregnancy.

Whatever maybe your terminology or reason, you are only but redefining evil. Get it clearer; an abortion for whatsoever reason is nothing but a human sacrifice to the god of self. That a baby is not convenient for you or you do not want it, you are too young, you cannot afford it, it is a girl but you wanted a boy is just the epitome of pure human selfishness and wickedness; a tragic truth about our evil excuses for murder. We seem to have forgotten that unwanted pregnancies are most often the result of sex that was wanted.

We are really so disbelieving that we fail to realize that the same God who creates the child and determines its time of conception is also the very one who blesses us and provides our needs:1 Samuel. 2:7-8; Matthew 6:8; Luke 12:30; Philippians. 4:19. Abortion is evil because what is happening in the womb is the unique life-forming work of God. To attack and kill the human being in the womb is to assault God. God is making the child. God is weaving a unique image of his divine glory with the purpose of imaging forth that glory in the world. Killing that child is just a direct attack on God's glory.

The unborn are not regarded impersonally in the Bible. They are regarded as people, they are regarded with honor, and any honest reading of the Bible should make it abundantly clear about how God views abortion. Please help rescue those being led away to death; hold back those staggering toward slaughter for they are innocent.

They meant no harm, they committed no crime. If you say, "but we knew nothing about this," does not he who weighs the heart perceive it? Does not he who guards your life know it? Will he not repay each person according to what he has done? (Proverbs 24:11-12). Isaiah said, cry it aloud, spare it not, lift up your voice like a trumpet, show my people their transgression, and the house of Jacob their sins. The one who avenges murder has remembered oppressed people. He has never forgotten their cries.

And if you are in one of the situations mentioned above and still wonder if you should have an abortion, I pray that the following verses from the Bible will help you make your decision.

God is the owner of life. He formed the man from the dust of the ground and breathed into his nostrils the breath of life, and the man became a living being (Genesis-2:7).

Job said "You gave me life and showed me kindness, and in your providence watched over my spirit (Job 10:12). David said "Know that the Lord is God. It is he, who made us, and we are his; we are his people, the sheep of his pasture (Psalm 100:3). Yet you brought me out of the womb; you made me trust in you even at my mother's breast. From birth I was cast upon you; from my mother's womb you have been my God (Psalm 22:9-10). For you created my inmost being; you knit me together in my mother's womb.

I praise you because I am fearfully and wonderfully made; your works are wonderful, I know that full well. My frame was not hidden from you when I was made in the secret place. When I was woven together in the depths of the earth, your eyes saw my <u>unformed body</u>. All the days ordained for me were written in your book before one of them came to be (Psalm 139:13-16). This is what the Lord says, he who made you, who formed you in the womb, and who will help you... (Isaiah 44:2).

Listen to me, O house of Jacob, all you who remain of the house of Israel, you whom I have upheld since you were <u>conceived</u>, and have carried since your birth. Even to your old age and gray hairs I am he, I am he who will sustain you. I have made you and I will carry you; I will sustain you and I will rescue you (Isaiah 46:3-4). And now the Lord says—he who formed me in the womb to be his servant to bring Jacob back to him and gather Israel to himself, for I am honored in the eyes of the Lord and my God has been my strength (Isaiah 49:5). The word of the Lord came to me, saying, "Before I formed you in the womb I knew you, before you were born I set you apart; I appointed you as a prophet to the nations" (Jer. 1:4-5).

Having seen that the giver and creator of human life is God, obviously he would be displeased at its ungrateful destruction. In the book of Exodus 21verses 22 and 23 we read that if some men were fighting and they caused injury to a pregnant woman, they were to be punished. If they caused her to lose her child, they were to be put to death. From this law that God gave Israel, we see that God not only viewed an unborn child as a living person, but that anybody responsible for its death was accountable for murder.

Though evil is redefined, the Word of God surpasses human reasoning without exclusion. Life is a gift of God and should be cherished, nourished and protected. Despite the fact that the Bible does not specifically use the word "abortion," nowhere in the Bible does it say "Thou shall not abort your children." but it's clear about "murder."Abortion is murder. You shall not murder (Exodus 20:13).

One of the key themes throughout the Bible is that Christians should be concerned about the welfare of the poor, weak and helpless. It is our duty to defend the cause of the weak and fatherless; mainly the rights of the poor and oppressed. We are to rescue the weak and needy; deliver them from the hand of the wicked.

Christians should support groups working to make abortion unacceptable in our countries, donate their time and money to pregnancy care centers. And above all pray that God will change the hearts of those promoting genocide in our nations. How old and how new is evil! Was it not evil among politicians and religious leaders that brought Christ to Pilate before the soldiers who beat Him to exhaustion, forced Him under the heavy cross, drove nails into His body and made Him a common criminal to die on the cross with thieves?

Sure, same people whose insatiable appetites are getting overdue attention. They rule based on an "old boys" network that puts high value on connections, loyalty and back scratching to unsavory practices that have routinely failed the critical sniff test of successive good governments in our various countries.

They belch contentedly from good meals daily with expanding bellies, riding the best cars while there are chronic shortages of basic services to the local people-electricity, medical, clean water, food, transportation and educational facilities. The same name tag! In their mist, a convicted murderer can easily bribe his way through the Supreme Court; subsequently an innocent fellow suffers his capital punishment. Just like Pilate acknowledged that Christ was innocent but willingly compromised with evil wishes and released a notorious ruffian and murderer; Barnabas. They are nothing but scoundrels hiding under the umbrella of patriotism. How many innocent citizens have been executed? How many are imprisoned simply because a corrupt-minded cop and government fabricated false evidence and witness against him in other to conceal a vital truth.

Yes, it is happening even now with money buying over justice, the poor are simply left out of luck. Restitution is the answer for the rich man's crime while severe imprisonment or even death sentence faces offence of the poor. Equality of all citizens becomes impossible especially when financial status is a factor.

Since the wealthy criminal receives a lighter sentence simply because he offers to pay some fine, evil must continue for if money solved the problem before, money will solve it again. The word is clear; you shall do no injustice in judgment: you shall not be partial to the poor, nor show favoritism to the great; but you shall judge your neighbor in righteousness.

We are truly getting along with evil, occult symbolism and practices are so widespread that they have become part of everyday life. I am aware that it may be hard for you to believe but you can determine it for yourself that from a box of matches you bought to the latest car has an occult emblem on them. Psychics no longer need to hide they practices from public view. Many evil folks are no longer being considered as charlatans but, rather, they are being upheld as significant contributors to societies needs. It is all about money, kill the children and feed their fathers with the blood money, kill the fathers and feed their children with the blood money.

Fill their blood with drugs, adulterated food and fake drugs; exploit them for slavery, prostitution and hard labor. Seal their father's mouth with money but if he rejects, bribe the police on your way, settle with the custom officers and call the politician when it gets tough. Of course your lawyer is always there to turnaround the white truth. Pay him to kill every eye witness and destroy all the evidence. Offer him a huge amount of money so that the hand of a man will be judge for that of a monkey. Finally, clap for the lawyer for his bravery and eloquence. Wherever evil is concealed, peace is on the run for darkness and light are incompatible.

How can these inconsistencies in Christianity be unstitched; being both evil-ridden, salt and light; being both a spring of disillusionment and illumination at the same time? It is really ugly! To my intensive review of the Scripture, marital unfaithfulness {including adultery, prostitution, fornication, pornography, and incest} as instructed by Jesus in Matthew 5 verses 32 and 19 verses 9 and having a non Christian spouse as used by Apostle Paul in 1 Corinthians 7 verses 15 are the only two biblical reasons that warrant God's permission for divorce and remarriage.

Nowadays we divorce each other not necessary because of unfaithfulness but for legal rights, conditional love, for the alimony the court grants or because we no longer find him/her attractive. Subsequently, we marry a former boy/girl friend. So what! The law grants it. It is upsetting that the divorce rate among professing Christians is nearly as high as that of the unbelieving world. People divorce and remarry even in the same church.

They are interested in justifying their divorces, they approve it, defend it, advocate for it; even the some churches bless it by refusing to discipline the members who divorce and by receiving those who have divorced into their fellowship. They approve it simply by remaining silent and accepting the sinner who has wickedly divorced his/her spouse.

God clearly declared in the book of Malachi 2 verse 16; I hate divorce. God's plan is that marriage should be a lifetime commitment for they are no longer two, but one. He is not saying that you've got to simply bear the worse and fulfill your marriage vows but there are other preferred options.

Divorce is not an option for any married Christian whose marriage is troubled. I believe the wisest thing that God would ask us all to do if possible would be to pray for wisdom, grace, and strength to forgive to help bring the fallen spouse into full repentance and forgiveness but not divorce. The only way out of any troubled marriage is not on the filthiness of our human law but on repentance, confession of sins, forgiveness, reconciliation, having the will to love, submission and changed behavior.

But, if the adulterous spouse will not give up his or her infidelity or wishes to leave, it may be necessary to let the adulterous spouse go. No person can be unfaithful to his or her spouse without first being unfaithful to God at heart. To deny love to one's spouse is to refuse to love someone Jesus loves, and to deny love to one's spouse is to deny love to Jesus Christ Himself.

In this age, one is free to pursue almost any lifestyle, provided he rattles off the appropriate number of "forgive us our trespasses as we forgive those who trespassed against us, if we say we have no sin we made thee a liar or we are like fishes in the river we cannot deny water." Provided he pays his tithe, sows seed of faith or donates to the Church fund, he is a good brother. He may have slept with almost all the sisters in the Church; possibly he is the praise leader of the Church. So what, nobody cares! For how long do we watch evil propagate? Why do we fold our arms and watch this world dancing joyfully towards destruction?

A concern about this rising tide of secularism and evil in our societies is highly needed. All that Jesus, Daniel, and John's Revelation foretold are soon coming to fulfillment in a swift. We are towards the harvest of the "wheat" and the "tares."

..The Bible gives reference to a great end time world harvest of the wheat and tares that will occur at the end of this age. It explains that the wheat is God's people and that the tares are Satan's people. The angels of God have been instructed to let the wheat and tares grow up together until the harvest at the end of the age. At that time the angels will be instructed to gather the wheat into God's barn and to bundle the tares together to be burned.

Common sense dictates that a wheat harvest takes place when the ripe wheat in the field is at peak. Thus, the harvest of the wheat and the tares occur when the greatest numbers of real Christians are dwelling on the earth. The time for the wheat harvest can be known by observing Christianity in the world. This is one reason why the Bible tells us that the season of the return of Jesus will be known to those who are watching for it.

Therefore, it is very pressing today that we search out from Scripture the true nature and functions of a true Christian, discover the dynamic power of the early church and apply them in this present life just as we cross the doorsill which divides the twentieth and twenty-first centuries.

The world seems to be a terribly complicated place, especially when compared with the world of the early church. And yet, there is no reason why Christianity in this twenty-first century should not be what it was in the first century. True Christianity operates on exactly the same basis now as it did then. The same power which turned the world upside-down in the book of Acts is available to us today. What kept us from experiencing that power today?

I believe the major barrier we face is *ignorance*. Most Christians are tragically unaware of the biblical pattern for a practical Christian living. Some will only remember the existence and wickedness of Satan when there is a fatal accident, plane clash, sudden death, natural disaster, sicknesses, and loss of money, loss of properties, retard business, barrenness of life or any other tragedy occurrences.

Others remember his works only when a possessed is delivered or in a funeral ceremony but when things goes right, this sinful and corrupted world prepared for fire turns to be a happier place. Even true Christians, the true "wheat," still vainly attempt to do what their Master instructed. Some go to Church simply because it is Sunday or that it has been imbibed in them right from childhood. So, they've become hopeless and counterproductive, swapping the divine knowledge with mundane tactics. (See Matt. 13:24-30).

We need to realize that elements of true and false Christianity will be intermingled in the same world, in the same church, even in the same person. And any careless attempt to get rid of the false runs the risk of uprooting the true as well. Our goal as Christians should not be to go on a search and destroy mission against all the evil in the world, but to do everything we can to make the

"WORD" in us so strong and healthy that the enemies outside are powerless to damage it.

Now is not the time for Christians to remain ignorant. Christians lose their power simply because they lose interest in their Bibles. They would rather read Christian fiction, romance novels, prophetic fiction, and watch season 1-4 of every movie, only to keep themselves from knowing the word of God. Satan himself has gotten Christians to believe that they don't need God's Word. I can say this dogmatically because of the condition Christianity is in right now. If the same amount of Christians would study their Bibles as much as they read residual or other worthless materials, there would be a mighty army and this world would know that the church of God is alive and well on planet Earth.

Our ignorance is not a badge of honor but a symbol of shame and weakness. We need to get back to the Scriptures and regain the strength we once had. It is a shame that ungodly religions are making their ways into every part of the world while Christians are wallowing in the mud. It is a shame that we slumber while evil propagates. This is why Christianity is being overrun by false religions, Sodomites, anti-Christian sentiment and evil laws.

Nowadays, a Christian can confidently recite the names of all football leagues, name all the football players; their clubs and match allowances but he cannot recite just five verses of the scriptures. A Christian can stay awake all night just to watch football but dozes off the very hour he stepped into the Church. When was the last time you read the Minor Prophets, better yet when was the last time you read John 3:15 or 17?

When was the last time you sat at supper as a family and discussed spiritual issues rather than discussing your arrogant 11 year old son's useless sports trophies? Have you ever heard your son say that he would like to be like Peter in the Bible or do you see him moving in the direction of wanting to be a movie star? The sad fact is that majority of Christians are biblically ignorant by design. Their refusal to grow in the grace and knowledge of the

Lord Jesus Christ is a sad commentary on our day. No, you can't become biblically astute by reading your Bible's paperback.

The problem Christians face is one of remaining righteously indignant toward evil. Peter described Lot as one who was, "... sore distressed by the lascivious life of the wicked for that righteous man dwelling among them, in seeing and hearing, vexed his righteous soul from day to day with their lawless deeds:" 2 Peter 2:7-8. Initially, the evil of wicked men distresses and vexes our righteous souls.

But now, the prolonged exposure to the lascivious life of the wicked causes our consciences to become abrasive. Sinners are no longer afraid in Zion, a Christian unashamedly discusses his sexual encounter with prostitutes and dogs with no sign of remorse .Over time, we are growing accustomed to the evil around us. We 'adjust' and there is no more adverse reaction. We can invite adultery, fornication, nakedness, cursing and blasphemy of God into our homes and are not shocked by it. We sit with our children and watch nude movies yet we call it entertainment.

Sin is portrayed as fun, excitement and a mind enhancing growth experience. The many influences that surround us now are so powerful and at times almost overwhelming to those not strong in their faith. The "everybody is doing it" or "it doesn't matter" syndrome has eaten deep into our bones and marrows.

Parents no longer question their children about ill-gotten wealth just because they want to show off in public meeting. We allow the homosexual life style to go unchallenged, legalization of same-sex marriage; gay and lesbian couples are granted full to marriage right even in some churches and we say, "If they want to live that way, it's no skin off my teeth." We have become street-wise and speak of illicit sex, drug abuse and every sort of wickedness with ease. It is evident that Christians have become desensitized to sin.

Even the church that is meant to encourage its members to make spiritual progress, and to show their faith by their behavior, both through their ethics and their good works, to administer brotherly correction when someone errs and emphasizing that followers should be spiritually united with Christ and with each other, have demonstrated an amazing ability to overlook many biblical virtues and allowed denominational fragmentation and bickering to weaken it.

A demon possessed can be a member of a Church for years without being delivered, a demon possessed can be a chorister, a demon possessed can be an usher in the church even a member of the Church council, Deacon or Deaconess; because the Church now spends too much time splitting doctrinal hairs, separating, and then hiding in her self righteousness designed to keep its members comfortable and safe in the inducted doctrines. On the outside, the world is going to hell while on the inside; we are playing the religion game called "Church Politics".

The Church is now comfortably dwelling in luxury, aggressively pursuing money as if it is a secular enterprise. Churches now have VCRs, air-conditioners, remote controls, and fast food joints, central air conditions, great sound systems, well-educated preachers, plush pews, fine-tuned choirs, pianos, and organs. We are blessed with committees, plans, and money.

In fact, we have so many churches that we are guaranteed to find one to suit any whim or preference. It is happening so today in Christian circles, with pulpits disappearing, suits and ties seemingly too bothersome, and choirs sounding decidedly more like entertainers than worshipers. In the struggle to win more Church members, Christians are entrapped in a thousand worldly schemes of evangelism because the more members, more money for the Pastor. The world has become churchier and the church has become worldlier that in many cases it is difficult to tell them apart.

Pastors now preach prosperity sermons; messages are no longer from the heart of God while 'thus says the Lord' is now the thing of the 19adams. In all too often, the messages are pleasant but cannot make our hearts ache for our sins not even the lost turn to

Christ. The church is now more conscious in raising millionaires than soul hunters.

And what does the devil and his demons see in all these? Do they see a visible Church full of power, sacrifice, love, forgiveness, and people who consider others more important than themselves? I think, not! They see polished televangelists with perfect hair and smiles pulling the wool over the eyes of countless thousands of gullible people as they ask for offerings, tithes and seed of faith.

They see models and superstars rather than preachers, those who parades assorted suits of thousands of dollars with expensive shoes which it cost may feed majority of their members for a year; pulpit politicians. They see the hypocrisy of moral uprightness proclaimed proudly in word and contradicted in deed. They see a denominationally fragmented church that cannot even clean its own house, let alone agree enough to present a united front. Let's forget about the Church for now, I will address their irresponsibility later.

It is the Christian's responsibility not to be conformed to this world. (Rom. 12:2) What more incentive do we need to correct these spiritual impairments than the Word of God? What more do we need for prosperity if not seeking first the Kingdom of God and his righteousness? Believers should have an inherent desire to understand the Savior's will and to please Him. To know His will is simply to know His Word and adjust our lives to it.

True worshippers should be reminded of whom they ought to be, reminded of the shortness of time and nearness of our Lord's return. The apostle exhorts us to "redeem the time, because the days are evil." What does it mean to "redeem the time"? It means to "rescue from loss." Lost time can never be recovered. All of us have been guilty of wasting time, and we all have regrets, over time we could have spent more wisely. So the apostle tells us not to waste time nor lose time, but rather make good use of the time "because the days are evil." He says the days are such that we have no time to lose. The day in which we live should cause us to spend our time more wisely.

Therefore, it is time for Christians to keep close to the word of God, watching keenly against all who seek to bewilder, deceive and destroy them. A state of apostasy is worse than a state of ignorance. Let us not compromise evil upon the good way of God, false charge against the way of truth must be exposed to the heaviest condemnation. How dreadful is the state of Christianity? Yet, though our failure is deplorable it is not utterly hopeless. The leper can be made clean, the blind can see and even the dead may be raised for our hope is restored in Christ Jesus.

Jabez was born in pain and acquainted with sorrow. You can imagine what it was like growing up with your name meaning pain. In spite of his contagious beginning, he determined to be different from his siblings. He knew that his problem was not incurable but wanted an everlasting and permanent solution; then God changed him. In the book of I Chronicles 4:10 he said- "Oh, that You would bless me indeed, and enlarge my territory, that your hand would be with me, and that you would keep me from evil, that I may not cause pain." Is thy wickedness a grief to thee? Believe in the Lord Jesus, and thou shall be saved.

Satan is very much aware that the weakest soul who abides in Christ is more than a match for the hosts of darkness, and that, should he reveal himself openly, he would be met and resisted. Therefore he seeks to draw away the soldiers of the cross from their strong fortification, while he lies in ambush with his forces, ready to destroy all who venture upon his ground. Only in humble reliance upon God, and obedience to all His commandments, shall we be secure.

For that reason, Christians need to see the challenges of this very hour, and realize that we have been uniquely called to do the only thing that counts in this day and age. Running or hiding from it cannot save us; for as much as we are in this Heavenly race, discerning the tricks of the devil, whose agents so surround us, language is so plausible, manners are so insinuating, appearance is often so imposing, arguments are so subtle, activities are so unwearied, insight into our weaknesses is so keen, enmity against Christ and His gospel is so implacable, lack of all principle and all honesty is so thorough, and his net may be drawing around us is very imperative. To make Heaven, overcoming Satan and his cohorts is a MUST!

But it flummoxes me seeing Christians verbally honoring the word of God. They do not study the Bible very much rather preferred to be fed and nourished through a second-hand source: sermons, radio and television sermons, books; anything but the Bible itself. They are perfectly contented to let others do the praying and fasting for them. And when it comes to demons, many prefer not to hear about them.

These atmospheres of ignorance and unbelief have destroyed many churches and lives. Just like a rich Christian brother wrote his daily prayers on the wall right opposite his bed. Whenever he wakes up in the morning or going to bed at night, he simply points to the wall saying" God that is my prayer", so had the lips of many Christians grown heavy! Unavoidably, every "Child of God" has a duty to do warfare against the enemy.

Practically, it is either we put on the weapons of our warfare and fight, as the word of God commands us or we face the risk and danger of being daily defeated and eventually destroyed by our arch enemy. Many are being destroyed because they do not know how sophisticated the enemy is: those who knew were not properly taught on how to fight him. Unfortunately, devil does not even exempt any body no matter your rank or level in the faith.

So, why do Christians slightly despise and neglect a being that planned mutiny to overthrow our Almighty God? A being that boldly, fearlessly and deceitfully tempted Our Savior Jesus Christ for three good times and he valiantly withheld the answered prayers of Daniel for good 21 days. He boldly went to the presence of God asking for permission to torment one of the champions of righteousness, Job. Yes, he indefatigably tempted Job in all his earthly possession even to the point of death but Job understood all his devices.

This same vicious enemy really hates us and he is working tirelessly to steal, kill and destroy those under his influence. Jesus said to Peter in Luke 22:31 "Simon, Simon Satan has asked excessively that you be given up to him, out of the power and keeping of God that he might sift you like grain". Take a pause and ponder over this figurative expression "excessively" and "sift you like grain".

The former means that Satan never rest; he is tirelessly seeking our destruction while the latter means to remove all your air-conditioners, every bit of comfort around you and make you sweat big time. It means to remain just the bone after he had utterly destroyed your flesh.

It means to replace your happiness with sorrow and sickness, bringing you down to ash from your present throne and glory. Thus ignoring such tireless crook is the worst heedlessness and negligence ever.

OPERATION DIVIDE AND CONQUER

When Satan wants to hinder or destroy you, he will try to plant someone that will become a hindrance by stopping your walk with God, by causing you to sin, by causing your vision to be divided, by confusing the vision or slowing down your momentum and by wearing you out with mental weariness. Mental weariness is what Job faced after enduring so many things only to have his wife tell him to 'curse God and die' (Job 2:9).Job's wife voluntarily wanted to become a widow.

His three friends told him he has sinned while he was sitting there with boils all over his body. Everyone attacked him instead of someone coming to stand with him. They were accusing him of hypocrisy, of having secret sin, of having done something to loose God's favor.

Even till now, the only way to overcome mental depression is to get into the presence of God. Sometimes it takes weeping in God's presence to refresh you. When you weep before God,

He turns toward you. You won't get victory by going somewhere, watching TV, or some fleshly thing, but only by getting in His presence, for a broken and contrite heart brings His peace and release.

I vividly remember the very man of God, power packed. Who, after a wonderful sermon one certain Sunday, declared to his congregation saying " tell the devil I' m above fornication, tell the devil I' m untouchable" yes the hungry congregation echoed 'amen' but it was not long thereafter, the Pastor committed fornication and abortion with his village house maid. As his reputation washed out, his members began to seek him out, sometimes waiting days for them to hear his confession.

How would he heal their illnesses or speak directly to their sins again? This Pastor began to be attacked, sometimes physically and, at other times emotionally and psychologically. He was verbally mocked, scorned, and abused. Though not everyone was so pleased, but this eventually crippled his Ministry in that environment. What a sorry pity? But that is a tip of the sophisticated nature of Satan.

He uses a sophisticated dialectic process or a very emotional interaction and resolution between multiple Biblical paradigms or ideologies to raise the pressure to compromise and yield to temptations. Refined for our times, it was first demonstrated in the Garden of Eden. Look at the dialogue in Genesis 3:1-5 and ponder on the familiar subtle process he began with:

Now the serpent was more cunning than any beast of the field which the Lord God had made. And he said to the woman, "Has God indeed said, 'you shall not eat of every tree of the garden?" And the woman said to the serpent, "We may eat the fruit of the trees of the garden; but of the fruit of the tree which *is* in the midst of the garden, God has said, 'You shall not eat it, nor shall you touch it, lest you die.'

Then the serpent said to the woman, "You will not surely die. For God knows that in the day you eat of it your eyes will be opened and you will be like God, knowing good and evil." So when the woman saw that the tree *was* good for food, that it *was* pleasant to the eyes, and a tree desirable to make one wise, she took of its fruit and ate. She also gave to her husband with her, and he ate. Then the eyes of both of them were opened, and they knew that they *were* naked; and they sewed fig leaves together and made themselves coverings. And they heard the sound of the Lord God walking in the garden in the cool of the day, and Adam and his wife hid themselves from the presence of the Lord God among the trees of the garden. Then the Lord God called to Adam and said to him, "Where are you?"

So he said, "I heard your voice in the garden, and I was afraid because I was naked; and I hid myself." And He said, "Who told you that you *were* naked? Have you eaten from the tree of which I commanded you that you should not eat?" Then the man said, "The woman whom you gave *to be* with me, she gave me of the tree, and I ate. And the Lord God said to the woman, "What *is* this you have done?" The woman said, "The serpent deceived me, and I ate."

One day a Sister walked up to me, "Brother Josiah please I want to ask you some questions, can we talk privately she said". We went to a corner, and then she asked, please brother, is masturbation sin? I answered, yes! But immediately, I sensed what was coming, emotions was! There is nothing wrong with this question but it might be an emotional trap of the devil. When one is having an emotional problem in their marriage, the devil might send someone to start telling them, "Boy if I had a husband or wife like you, I'm sure,   I would take good care of you and not treat you like your spouse does. Oh, I do know and understand what you're going through and I want to help you." My goodness', I have never met a man/woman like you in my whole life; you are so caring and kind. Oh! My brother you are talented; my sister you sang like an angel: admiration!

And the next thing you know, they get into a relationship and their marriage is really ruined. The kids are caught in the middle and it is a complete mess, because Satan's strategy is to use others to divide and conquer you. So when Satan wants to destroy you or me, it is almost always through a person he will send into your life. This is the reason why, it is necessary that you discern the relationships you get involved with and discern the people you hang around with. Satan can send someone to fill a void in your life, someone that appears to meet your emotional needs.

Someone who will understand your situation better than anyone else, that is why the Bible calls him 'the master of intrigues'. He does not come with machine guns and armored tanks for then you would easily recognize him as an enemy; but he comes in a subtle and cunning way that might seem harmless that if you are not aware of his tricks, you would be swept off feet in a twinkle of an eye.

The demonic realm has authority in this physical world; even the Bible speaks more about demons than angels. Thus it takes more than a bench warmer in the Church to understand that demonic authority is subject to the authority we have in Christ. Probably it is because of the extreme importance of correct understanding of our divine privileges and responsibilities; for the power which the Word confers on a militant believer, so the enemy has specially sought to hold back this knowledge from God's people.

He has been successful through the employment of the blinding tactics, which he has found effective in the case of the lost, and of those who believe not. (2 Corinthians 4: 3, 4) We are to give ourselves to it through Jesus Christ our Lord, standing firmly against every manipulation of this enemy.

These cannot be essentially carried out when we deliberately have decided to dwell in ignorance. The word is designed to perfect the man of God, that he may be perfect, completely furnished unto every good work thus we have the power, a bona fide authority to handle the problems and attacks which pursue us on every facet of life but only few realize and use it.

David understood warfare and he knew who the enemy was. In Psalm 139:21-24 he stated, "Do I not hate them, O Lord, who hate you? And am I not grieved and do I not loathe those who rise up against you? I hate them with perfect hatred; they have become my enemies." David was correct in hating God's enemies and we see his heart as he goes on and cries out to God in verse 23.

Apostle Paul also when writing to his friends in Corinth, from the city of Ephesus, says. I, Paul, myself entreat you, by the meekness and gentleness of Christ -- I who am humble when face to face with you but bold to you when I am away! -- I beg of you that when I am present I may not have to show boldness with such confidence as I count on showing against some who suspect us of acting in worldly fashion. For though we live in the world we are not carrying on a worldly war, for the weapons of our warfare are not worldly but have divine power to destroy strongholds. {2 Corinthians 10:1-4}

"For though we walk (or live) in the flesh, we do not war according to the flesh." Finally, He concluded Ephesians 6 talking about warfare. He said in verse 10, "Be strong in the Lord [be empowered through your union with Him]; draw your strength from Him [that strength which His boundless might provides].11) Put on God's whole armor [the armor of a heavy-armed soldier which God supplies], that you may be able successfully to stand up against [all] the strategies and the deceits of the devil. 12) For we are not wrestling with flesh and blood [contending only with physical opponents], but against the despotisms, against the powers, against [the master spirits who are] the world rulers of this present darkness, against the spirit forces of wickedness in the heavenly (supernatural) sphere.

13) Therefore put on God's complete armor, that you may be able to resist and stand your ground on the evil day [of danger], and, having done all [the crisis demands], to stand [firmly in your place]. 14) Stand therefore [hold your ground], having tightened the belt of truth around your loins and having put on the breastplate of integrity and of moral rectitude and right standing with God, 15) And having shod your feet in preparation [to face the enemy with the firm-footed stability, the promptness,

and the readiness produced by the good news] of the Gospel of peace. 16) Lift up over all the [covering] shield of saving faith upon which you can quench all the flaming missiles of the wicked [one].

17) And take the helmet of salvation and the sword that the Spirit wields, which is the Word of God. 18) Pray at all times (on every occasion, in every season) in the Spirit, with all [manner of] prayer and entreaty. To that end keep alert and watch with strong purpose and perseverance, interceding in behalf of all the saints (God's consecrated people)." These scriptures cover it all. It explains who the battle is with, and describes the levels of power of the enemy; then Paul goes on to explain how to battle, when to stand, and how to pray; and most importantly we cannot battle without the Lord. Why then should we fight ignorantly?

NATURE HUMILIATES US

Our human strategies are founded upon limited human understanding and the best estimates human beings can make. The sociologist impugns environmental background or living conditions and has applied a holistic approach into helping us solve problems and enhance our potentials within near environments but our problems seem too far from social solutions.

The psychologist suggests the mindset and has tried helping us manage our mind to understand how we could deal with this systematic breakdown of our focus; negative thoughts can possibly affect positive realities, they said. But our problems are more of supernaturally initiated than mind management.

The health Practitioners deduce the way we feel but no medication could cure death, the ordinaries disparage the government; riots and demonstrations are mere formalities, politicians censure the bad economic influence created by opposing parties: while Christians and some other religions point finger at Satan. Fundamentally, these evils are undefeatable not by their nature but by our approach.

The book of Isaiah vividly figures the desolation that follows when people turn their backs on the living God. Your habitation will lie desolate, your cities are burned with fire, your efforts shall be fruitless, your focus shall be confused and in your very presence enemies devours your land; it is desolate as overthrown by enemies, and the children of your youth are left like a booth in a vineyard, like a lodge in a cucumber field; a besieged city.

However, Christ is the water of life, which refreshes any soul that receives Him but many choose to spread and promote iniquity and are set fort as restless because there is no peace for the wicked. As cloud hinders the light of the sun, so do these darken counsel by words wherein there is no truth! Seeing that you increase darkness in this world, it is justified that darkness should be your portion now even in the afterlife.

In the midst of our talk of liberty and development, we are the vilest slaves to nature; our own lust has gained a complete victory over us, and we are actually in bondage. When we are entangled, we are easily defeated. But how do believers who love the Lord Jesus Christ come to deny Him, Matt.10: 33; 2 Tim.2: 12.

How do believers end up making themselves "enemies of the cross of Christ" (Phil.3: 18-19). This is not part of our calling and I pray, May it not be the fulfillment of prophecy on us.

We begot our predicament and quandary. The cause of all failures in man is the triplet sin of unbelief, pride, ignorance or refusal to submit to God's will. Mankind has been failing God, himself and other creatures right from the dispensation of innocence where he lost paradise to this present dispensation of grace. Ever since the lost, we have tried unsuccessfully to recoup this dominion but the very key solution to our problems lies with us day in and out while we deliberately have chosen to wander in wilderness of ignorance.

Regardless of all advancement in technology and science, nature still humiliates us with earthquakes, storms, tsunamis, avalanche, fire, famine, flood, hail, heat, hurricane, limnic eruption, landslide, mudslide, sinkhole, solar flare, storm surge, thunderstorm, tornado, volcanic eruption, waterspout and winter storm. An attempt to control these brings greater disaster like pollution, global warming, and assorted dreadful sicknesses to mention but a few. A glance at our yesterdays would be convincible to shed tears for humankind.

The January 23, 1556 earthquake in Shaanxi, China killed 830,000 persons, August 17, 1668 earthquake in Anatolia, Turkey killed 8,000 persons, November 1, 1755 earthquake in Lisbon, Portugal killed 80,000 persons, January 9, 1857 earthquake in Fort Taejon, California killed 1 person, December 16, 1857 earthquake in Naples, Italy killed 11,000 person, April 3, 1868 earthquake in Hilea, Hawaii, USA killed 77 persons, October 21, 1868 earthquake in Hayward, California, USA, killed 30 persons, March 26, 1872, earthquake in Owens Valley, California, USA killed 27,

August 31, 1886, earthquake in Charleston, S. Carolina, USA killed 60 persons, October 27, 1891, earthquake in Mino-Owari, Japan killed 7,273 persons, April 19, 1892, earthquake in Vacaville, California, USA, killed 1 person, June 12, 1897, earthquake in Assam, India killed 1500 persons, January 31, 1906, earthquake in Colombia Ecuador, killed 1,000 persons, April 18, 1906, earthquake in San Francisco, California, killed 3,000 persons, August 17, 1906, earthquake in Valparaiso, Chile, killed 20,000 persons.

December 28, 1908, earthquake in Messina & Reggio Calabria, Italy, killed 70,000 persons, October 11, 1918, earthquake in Puerto Rico, killed 116 persons, December 16, 1920, earthquake in Ningxia-Gansu, China, killed 200,000 persons, September 1, 1923, earthquake in Kant, Japan, killed 143,000 persons, June 29, 1925, earthquake in Santa Barbara, California, USA, killed 13 persons, March 7, 1927, earthquake in Tango, Japan, killed 3,020 persons, May 22, 1927, earthquake in Tsinghai, China, killed 200,000 persons, March 2, 1933, earthquake in Sanriku, Japan, killed 2,990 persons, March 11, 1933, earthquake in Long Beach, California, USA, killed 115 persons.

January 15, 1934, earthquake in Bihar, India, killed 10,700 persons, December 26, 1939, earthquake in Erzincan, Turkey, killed 32,700 persons, November 10, 1940, earthquake in Vrancea, Romania, killed 4,000 persons, December 7, 1944, earthquake in Tonankai, Japan, killed 1,223 persons, April 1, 1946, earthquake in Unimak Island, Alaska, USA, killed 165 persons, August 4, 1946, earthquake in Dominican Republic, killed 100 persons, December 20, 1946, earthquake in Nankaid.

Japan, killed 1,330 persons, August 15, 1950, earthquake in Assam Tibet, killed 1,526 persons, October 24, 1955, earthquake in Concord, California, USA, killed 1 person, December 4, 1957, earthquake in Govi-Altai Province, Mongolia, killed 30 persons, July 10, 1958, earthquake in Fair-weather, Alaska, USA, killed 5 persons, August 18, 1959, earthquake in Hebgen Lake, Montana, USA, killed 28 persons, February 29, 1960, earthquake in Agadir, Morocco, 10,000 persons.

May 22, 1960, earthquake in Valdivia, Chile, killed 5,700 persons, March 28, 1964, earthquake in Prince William Sound, Alaska, USA, killed 125 persons, June 16, 1964, earthquake in Niigata, Japan, killed 26 persons, April 29, 1965, earthquake in Seattle-Tacoma, Washington, USA, killed 7 persons, October 2, 1969, earthquake in Santa Rosa, California, USA, killed 1 person, May 31, 1970, earthquake in Peru, killed 66,000 persons, December 23, 1972, earthquake in Managua, Nicaragua, killed 6,000 persons.

February 4, 1975, earthquake in Haicheng, China, killed 10,000 persons, February 4, 1976, earthquake in Guatemala, killed 23,000 persons, July 27, 1976, earthquake in Tangshan, China, killed 242,419 persons, November 23, 1980, earthquake in Irpinia, Italy, killed 2735 persons, March 31, 1983, earthquake in Popayan, Cauca, SA, killed 197 persons, October 28, 1983, earthquake in Borah Peak, Idaho, USA, killed 2,

September 19, 1985, earthquake in Michoacán, Mexico, killed 9,500 persons, October 1, 1987, earthquake in Whittier Narrows, California, USA, killed 8, December 7, 1988, earthquake in

Spitak, Armenia, killed 25,000 persons, October 17, 1989, earthquake in Loma Prieta, California, USA, killed 63, June 28, 1991, earthquake in Sierra Madre, California, USA, killed 2, June 28, 1992, earthquake in Landers, California, USA, killed 3, September 2, 1992, earthquake in Nicaragua, killed 116, September 29, 1993, earthquake in Latur-Killari, India, killed 9,748 persons, January 17, 1994, earthquake in Northridge, California, USA, killed 60, June 9, 1994, earthquake in Bolivia, killed 5, January 17, 1995, earthquake in Kobe, Japan, killed 5,502 persons.

May 21, 1997, earthquake in Jabalpur, India, killed 38, July 17, 1998, earthquake in Guinea, killed 2,183 persons, January 25, 1999, earthquake in Colombia, killed 1,185 persons, August 17, 1999, earthquake in Zmit, Turkey, killed 17,118 persons.

In 1999, a 5.9 magnitude earthquake killed 143 people and left thousands homeless near Athens, Greece, September 20, 1999, earthquake in Chi-Chi, Taiwan, killed 2,400 persons, November 12, 1999, earthquake in Duzce, Turkey, killed 894,January 13, 2001, earthquake in Salvador, killed 844, January 26, 2001, earthquake in Gujarat, India, killed 20,085 persons June 23, 2001, earthquake in coastal Peru, killed 75, March 25, 2002, earthquake in Hindu Kush Region, Afghanistan, killed 1,000 persons, May 21, 2003, earthquake in Boumerdes, Algeria, killed 2,266 persons, December 22, 2003, earthquake in San Simeon, California, USA, killed 2, December 26, 2003, earthquake in southeastern Iran, killed 31,000 persons and March 28, 2005, earthquake in Northern Sumatra, Indonesia, killed 1,313 persons.

However, the seismological predictions could not salvage the occurrence of these natural failures. The Wellington avalanche on February 1910, an avalanche hit a small village of Blons near Bludenz Vorarlberg in Austrian Alps on 12 January 1954. Peru had the worst catastrophic natural disaster on May 31 1970 an undersea earthquake resulting from landslide. On February 23, 1999, the worst Alpine avalanche in 40 years killed 31 people in small Alpine village of Galtur, Austria.

The Kolka-Karmadon rock-ice slide occurred on the northern slope of the Kazbek massif in North Ossetia on September 20, 2002 following a partial collapse of the Kolka Glacier. Cyclone Sidr is the fourth named storm of the 2007 North Indian Ocean cyclone season. The storm eventually made landfall near Bangladesh on November 15 and caused large-scale evacuations. So far, 10,000 lives were claimed by the storm.

In 1970, a devastating tropical cyclone that struck East Pakistan (now Bangladesh) and India's West Bengal on November 12, 1970.It was the deadliest tropical cyclone ever recorded, and one of the deadliest natural disasters in modern times. Up to 500,000 people lost their lives in the storm, primarily because of the storm surge that flooded much of the low-lying islands of the Delta.

On the 29th April 1991 the same country experienced the deadliest tropical cyclones on record, a powerful tropical cyclone struck the Chittagong district of southeastern Bangladesh, killing at least 138,000 people and leaving as many as 10 million homeless.

The same was in 1963, 1961,1965,1960,1985 and 1988; killing 11520, 11468,19270,11149,11069 and 5,708 of Bangladeshis respectively. The 2004 Indian sub-duction Ocean earthquake occurred with epicenter off the west coast of Sumatra, Indonesia, which triggered a series of devastating tsunamis along the coasts of most landmasses bordering the Indian Ocean, killing more than 225,000 people in eleven countries including Indonesia, Sri Lanka, India and Thailand. The 2005 Kashmir Earthquake similar to 1906 San Francisco earthquake, 1935 Quetta earthquake and 2001 Gujarat earthquake occurred on 8 November 2005 killing nearly 73,276 Pakistani officials.

In July 17 2006, Indonesia experienced a Java earthquake. According to history, the Flooding of the Yellow River in northern China caused some of the highest death tolls in world history, with the 1887 Huang He flood killing 900,000 to 2,000,000 persons, the 1931 Huang He flood killed 1,000,000 to 4,000,000 persons the deaths was caused by the flooding include drowning, disease, ensuing famines, and droughts.

In the summer of 1998, China experienced massive flooding of parts of the Yangtze River, resulting in 3,004 dead, 14 million left homeless and $24 billion in economic loss. So was the Yellow River flood of 1911 killing 100,000 people, the 1938 Yellow River flood killed 500,000 to 700,000 people, the 1939 Tianjin flood killed 20,000 people, the 1948 Fuzhou flood killed 3,814 people, the 1951 Manchuria flood killed 4,800 people, the 1954 Yangtze river flood killed 30,000 people, the Banqiao Dam failure of 1975 killed 231,000 people, the 1981 Sichuan, Shanxi flood killed 2,075,the Sichuan flood of 1989 killed 3,814 people, the 1991 china flood mainly Sichuan, Guizhou, Hubei torrential floods mud-rock flows killed 1,723,Fujan,Anhui,Zhejiang flood killed 1,624 people. The same in 2004 and 2007 killing 1029 and 1348 people respectively.

In the year 2000, Mozambique experienced a natural disaster that killed 800 persons and 20,000 heads of cattle. This catastrophic flooding disaster was caused by heavy rainfall that lasted for five weeks and made many homeless. In 1984, Cameroon experienced a limnic eruption in Lake Monoun, which caused the deaths of 37 nearby residents.

The same was in 1986 when Lake Nyos erupted killing 1,700 people. The 2003 European heat wave was one of the hottest summers on record in Europe. The heat wave led to health crises in several countries and combined with drought to create a crop shortfall in Southern Europe. 35,000 people died because of the heat wave.

Most recently, cyclone Nargis killed nearly 50,000 Burmese on the May 3, 2008. The 1918 flu pandemic commonly referred to as the Spanish flu, a severe influenza that lasted from March 1918 to June 1920, spreading even to the Arctic and remote Pacific Islands. It is estimated that anywhere from 20 to 100 million people were killed worldwide.

The "Asian Flu" was category 2 flu pandemic outbreak of avian influenza that originated in China in early 1956 lasting until 1958.It originated from mutation in wild ducks combining with a pre-existing human strain. The virus was first identified in Guizhou. It spread to Singapore in February 1957, reached Hong Kong by April, and US by June. Death toll in the US was approximately 69,800.

Estimates of worldwide infection rate vary widely depending on source, ranging from 1 million to 4 million. What about the severe acute respiratory syndrome (SARS),a deadly respiratory disease in humans, which is caused by the SARS corona virus (SARS-COV), between November 2002 and July 2003, with 8,096 known infected cases and 774 death.

The AIDS epidemic was first identified by the U.S. Centers for Disease Control and Prevention in 1981, in 2007, an estimate of 33.2 million people lived with the disease worldwide and it killed an estimated 2.1 million people, including 330,000 children. To mention but a few, Civil wars, violent demonstrations and suicide bombers have claimed millions of lives. Amidst of all these deaths are professionals, Doctors, Scientist, lawyers, philosophers, Christians and Sinners. A very ugly yesterday and regretful today indeed! Our tears could not change it but we can affect our tomorrow now.

Truly, it calls for a careful consideration and examination for God did not make us to live this way, this destitute background and wretched living state were not created thus from the beginning, everything was made good for our use, consumption and total dominion. Rather our negative mindset and ignorance has reflected approach to solutions from the wrong perspectives thereby creating more harms in lieu of solution.

We have settled for the less, resorted to inordinate priorities and ambitions, yielding to failures though sometimes it is supernaturally initiated. Established authorities and powers like painted sepulchers and cankerworms rules selfishly for their wallets and personal objectives; amassing wealth limitlessly without civic accomplishment and good social reflection.

Wickedness is really at its zenith as Christians channels it to the signs of the end time. Whatever be the case, everyone yawns for rescue, cure and progress but the storming question is; who concocted these incurable tragedies of man? **The answer, Evil!**

~ 2 ~

<u>Evil</u>

Ignoring the cause of failure gives failure a renaissance

According to the comments of David Hume, a famous neo-skeptic philosopher of 18th century," Is God willing to prevent evil, but not able, then is He impotent. Is he able, but not willing? Then is He malevolent. Is He both able and willing? Whence then is evil? (Dialogues Concerning Natural Religion, Part X 1779). These are the yet unanswered questions of problem evil. Can we know the origin of evil? Does the presence of evil in this world really negate the existence of God? Is it possible to accommodate both the existence of God and the existence of evil within a coherent explanation of life?

There could hardly be more fundamental and perplexing questions. Seeing the work of evil, with its terrible results of woe and desolation, thus humanity question, how all these can exist under the sovereignty of one who is infinite in wisdom, power, and love. This is a mystery, of which a common human intellect finds no explanation but in our uncertainty and doubt, we are blinded to the truth plainly revealed in God's Word, and essential to salvation of our soul. Our problem with evil is not mainly ignorance of its cause but total negligence and ignorance of its cure, for we all acknowledge that sin resides in our heart but ignorance of the cure; the wholly good God in Christ, had made us desolate and miserable. For God was in Christ, reconciling the world unto himself, not imputing their trespasses unto them.... For He hath made Him to be sin for us, who knew no sin; that we might be made the righteousness of God in Him (2 Corinthians 5:19-21).

Prior to the manifestation of this evil, there was peace and joy throughout the universe, all were in perfect harmony with the Creator's will. Love for God was supreme, love for one another impartial not until the dilemma that brought the entire human race to this present state of humiliation, obliteration and death struck. Thus answering the question of where evil came from is still a disconcerted conundrum in the mind of many.

Scientifically, there is no substantial proof or idea of where evil emanated but there are realities of situations as seen in the Bible where an evil demon referred to as Satan or the devil manifested. Tragedies of our various experiences confirmed the existence of this wicked one as the Bible advised that all his effort is to kill, steal and destroy our souls. Evil and the evil one could be seen as two independent existences that have brought humanity to present execrable state.

Firstly, evil manifested itself as total selfishness, jealousy, disobedience and rebellion: aggressively pursuing the satisfaction of own desires and glory to the total disregard and detriment of health, well being, and lives of others. Tracing this Biblically, the devil was a creation of God, an angel who was at one time with God, trusted with enviable beauty, power, honor, wisdom and talents. Over the course of time, he grew restless of his possessions and wondered at the possibility of gaining more, and then suddenly he became jealous. He rebelled against God with his solicited army of many angels! God prevailed, so as a punishment for insurgency sent him and his armies out of Heaven to this earth.

This theory is based on the following scriptural references: please open your Bible with me, just be patient let's sort it out once and for all. **John 1 vs. 1-3:** "In the beginning was the Word and the Word was with God, and the Word was God. The same was in the beginning with God." He made all things; and without Him was not anything made that was made. **John 8 vs. 44:** "You belong to your father, the devil, and you want to carry out your father's desire. He was a murderer from the beginning, not holding to the truth, for there is no truth in him. When he lies he speaks his native language for he is a liar and father of lies." **Colossians 1 vs. 16-17:** "for by him all things were created: things in heaven and on earth, visible and invisible, whether thrones or power or rulers or authorities; all things were created by him and for him. He is before all things and in him all things hold together". **Jude 6** :And the angels who did not keep their positions of authority but abandoned their own home these he has kept in darkness, bound with everlasting chains for judgment on the great day".

II Peter 2 vs. 4: "for if God did not spare angels when they sinned, but sent them to, putting them into gloomy dungeons to be held for judgment".

I Timothy 3 vs. 6; he must not be a recent convert or he may become conceited and fall under the same judgment as the devil.

Isaiah 14 vs. 12 -15: How art thou fallen from heaven, O Lucifer, son of the morning! How art thou cut down to the ground, which didst weaken the nations! For thou hast said in thine heart, I will ascend into heaven, I will exalt my throne above the stars of God: I will sit also upon the mount of the congregation, in the sides of the north: I will ascend above the heights of the clouds; I will be like the most High. Yet thou shall be brought down to hell, to the sides of the pit. They that see thee shall narrowly look upon thee, and consider thee, saying, is this man that made the earth to tremble, that did shake kingdoms; that made the world as a wilderness, and destroyed the cities thereof; that opened not the house of his prisoners?"

Luke 10 vs. 18: He replied ...I saw Satan fall like lightning from heaven and **Revelation 12 vs. 7-9**: there was war in heaven. Michael and his angels fought against the dragon, and the dragon and his angels fought back. Nevertheless, he was not strong enough, and they lost their place in heaven. The great dragon was hurled down, that ancient serpent called the devil, Satan, who leads the whole world astray. He was hurled to the earth and his angels with him". These and other verses could be seen as substantial ground to establish that Satan was a creation of God as many theologians and Christians may view it, but let us critically cross-examine this fact to avoid profanation; remember that God knew the end from the beginning.

Some people assumed evil as a ruling force, a cosmic power, unknowable, impersonal, some kind of rational power in a Pre-Adamic world while others believed that God created everything including evil and the evil one as rightly stated above. He created evil for good purposes, because He wanted to affect some good purposes using evil, they said. I do not believe the former, as there is no Biblical verse or standard to institute the idea.

The latter also I do not accept because that could be a conjecture that Satan was created for falling and causing man to fall, being that God knew the end from the beginning. This is a perfidious idea that does not reveal God as a God of justice, love and holiness. It denies the omniscient nature of God; implies that God previously planned and purported the sinfulness and failures of man through Satan, thereby making Him [GOD] the Author or Instigator of Wickedness.

More so, suggesting that God has created a being that turned evil is to undermine the pureness of God's ability, mere understanding the gravity of impairment done by Satan to God's creation will render this fact confutative. The book of Matthew 7:18 declared that, a good tree cannot bear bad fruit, how then the bad fruit of Satan could have come from the good tree of God? Could the interpretation thereof be that God's creation would be imperfect?

Nonetheless, God saw everything that He had made, and behold they were very good according to Genesis 1 vs. 31. Then how and where does this evil thought of pride, disobedience and rebellion came into the mind of a good angel, Lucifer?

Contrarily, considering the book of Isaiah 14; also looking at these verses which said; "in the beginning was the Word and the Word was with God, and the Word was God. The same was in the beginning with God. All things were made by Him; and without Him was not anything made that was made says John 1 vs. 1-3". Another sustaining verse declare "for by Him were all things created, that are in heaven, and that are in earth, visible and invisible, whether they be thrones, or dominions or principalities or powers: all things were created by Him and for Him; and He is before all things and by Him all things consist Colossians 1 vs. 16-17".

Are you thinking about free moral agency? Let us have a look! *J Preston* penned the following: How true is the word, "O Lord, I know that the way of man is not in himself: it is not in man that walked to direct his steps" (Jer. 10:23). You have probably heard it said throughout all of your life, that MAN IS A FREE MORAL AGENT. Let me call attention to the fact that the phrase "free moral agent" is not a Scriptural one, any more than the term "rapture" is Scriptural. Free moral agency is simply a theological expression, man-manufactured for his convenience, and like most human inventions, and extra-biblical terminology, is not the truth at all. But briefly let us examine these three words: free moral agent.

An AGENT is an actor, one who is able to act or perform. **A FREE agent** is one who can act as he pleases without any restraint of any kind placed upon him. **A free MORAL** agent is one who is free to act as he pleases and without any restraint on all moral issues, that is all questions involving the qualities of right and wrong. I do not believe that the Bible anywhere teaches that man is a free moral agent. That teaching is a figment of the imagination of the harlot church system.

In fact, the Bible teaches the exact opposite. It tells us, "It is NOT of him that WILLETH or of him that runneth, but of GOD that showed mercy" (Rom. 9:16). The biggest lie that ever was told in human language is that all men are born free moral agents. They are not born free.

Be honest! Ask, Is that child free who is born in the slums; the child of a harlot and a whoremonger; a child without a name, who grows up with the brand of shame upon his brow from the beginning; who grows up amidst vice, and never knows virtue until it is steeped in vice? Is such a child a FREE MORAL AGENT, free to act intelligently, as he chooses, upon all moral questions? Is that child free who grows up amidst falsehood, and never knows what truth is until it is steeped in lies; that never knows what honesty is until it is steeped in crime? Is that child born free? Is that child free who is born in a communist land and in a godless home; who is told by its government and taught by its teachers that there is no God in heaven, and never knows even a verse of Scripture until it is steeped in unbelief and infidelity? Is that child born free? Is he a free moral agent? It is a sham, a delusion, and a snare to say it. It is not true. All are not born into this world as free moral agents. The truth is much stronger than that, for the fact is that NONE are free moral agents!

The preachers claim that when God made man in the first place, He endowed him with freedom of will, the ability to accept God's love or reject it, to keep God's laws or break them, and that the decision here and now is a final choice. But our Lord says, "No man can come unto me, except the Father which hath sent me draw him" (Jn. 6:44). Let us think a moment of just how free man is, how far his freedom reaches. A little observation and study will show that man's freedom has very narrow limits.

One is able to wish or desire or purpose as he pleases, but when he comes to carry out his wish or desire or purpose, he finds that he faces a problem. One is not free in the physical realm. Just let him try to jump off the Earth and land on Mars, for example. One is not free in the social realm. Not every man can marry the woman he wishes. One is not free in the economic realm.

Not every person who dreams of being a millionaire can become one, no matter how hard he tries. One is not free in the moral and spiritual realm. He may desire with all his being to rid the world of drunkenness and vice, of greed and hate and war, but who has yet accomplished that? Many are not able to free even themselves from a little weed called tobacco!

Life neither begins nor ends by choice and free will. Consider the matter of your own physical birth. What did you have to do with it, my friend? May I remind you that you were not consulted in the matter; you were absolutely passive in it; you had nothing whatsoever to do with it. You did not have a choice as to where or when you would be born. You had no choice as to what kind of a home or family you would be born into.

Did someone say to you, "Tell me, sir - or would you rather be madam? Would you like to have black hair, or blond hair, or perhaps no hair at all? Would you like to have brown eyes or blue? Would you like to have white skin, or black, or would green, or red, or yellow suit you better? And where would you like to live? In Miami, or Hong Kong, or Siberia, or maybe in the Congo, Nigeria or Tanzania?" Nothing of the sort! You were not even consulted. The sovereign Lord God of heaven and earth brought you into existence and ordained your path without so much a how-do-you-feel-about-it.

And you had no choice as to how you would be born, in what condition or state of being.

The Psalmist declared, "Behold, I was brought forth in a state of iniquity; my mother was sinful who conceived me and 1, too, am sinful" (Ps. 51:5, Amplified). Well did the apostle Paul write; by one man sin entered into the world, and death by sin; and so death passed upon all men, for that all have sinned ... for by one man's disobedience many were made sinners" (Rom. 5:12,19). If any man had brought himself into being, then we can conceive of the possibility of his having something to say about his condition and destiny. But mankind had absolutely nothing whatever to do with his coming into this world. It was the choice of God.

God chose to bring this creature into existence because He had a definite plan for him in His creative purposes in the whole universe. It was God who formed man of the dust of the ground.

It was God who breathed into his nostrils the breath of life. It was God who placed man in the Garden of Eden.

It was God who planted the tree of the knowledge of good and evil in the midst of the Garden. It was God who gave the law that man should neither touch this tree nor eat of it. And it was God who made the serpent and put him in the Garden and sent him along one beautiful day to tempt the man. It was GOD!

Even if Adam was a free moral agent, God is responsible for what happened in the Garden, for whatever a free moral agent may do, He is responsible for it who made him a free moral agent.

If God made man a free moral agent, then God created within man the propensities for either good or evil which determined his choices. If God made man a free moral agent, He knew beforehand what the result would be, and hence is just as responsible for the consequences of the acts of that free moral agent as He would be for the act of an irresponsible machine that He had made. Man's free moral agency, even if it were true, would by no means clear God from the responsibility of his acts since God is his Creator and has made him in the first place just what he is, well knowing what the result would be.

If God's will is ever thwarted, then He is not almighty. If His will is thwarted, then His plans must be changed, and hence He is not all-wise and immutable. If His will is never thwarted, then all things are in accordance with His will and He is the architect of all things as they exist. If He is all-wise and all-good, then all things, existing according to His will, must be working toward some wise and wonderful end!

"What shall we conclude then? Is there injustice on God's part? Certainly not! For He says to Moses, I will have mercy on whom I will have mercy and I will have compassion on whom I will have compassion. So then God's gift is not a question of human will and human effort, but of God's mercy. It depends not on ones own willingness ... but on God's having mercy on him. For the Scripture says to Pharaoh, I have raised you up for this very purpose of displaying My power in dealing with you, so that My name may be proclaimed the whole world over. So then He has mercy on whomever He wills (chooses) and He hardens--makes stubborn and unyielding of heart--whomever He wills.

You will say to me, why then does He still find fault and blame us for sinning? For who can resist and withstand His will? But who are you, a mere man, to criticize and contradict and answer back to God? Will what is formed say to him that formed it, why have you made me thus? Has the potter no right over the clay, to make out of the same mass one vessel for beauty and distinction and honorable use, and another for menial or ignoble and dishonorable use?" (Rom. 9:14-21).

It is a wicked and cruel lie to say that the unregenerated man is a "**free moral agent**." He is no such thing! He is a slave. "We know that the Law is spiritual; but I am a creature of the flesh (carnal), having been sold into slavery under the control of sin" (Rom. 7:14, Amplified).

The unregenerate man is a slave to sin. He is a slave to Satan. He is a slave of his own carnal mind and deceitfully wicked heart. He is a slave of his own vile passions. How can a man who is a slave and a captive of the devil be a "free moral agent"? Impossible! Adam sold us out. Adam gave us no choice in bringing his progeny under the workings of iniquity.

When Adam went into sin, he did not consult with any one of us as to our desire concerning anything he did. None of us had any power or any choice in the condition in which we entered this world. We were not sinners by choice, as we have erroneously been told. We are "born in sin, and sharpened in iniquity," with the carnal nature in us from the moment we leave the womb. Being "dead in trespasses and sins," dead to God, dead to truth, dead to purity, dead to reality, the Adamic race was no longer capable of making a choice or decision for salvation.

How truly the apostle wrote in Eph. 2:2-3, "And you were dead in trespasses and sins: wherein in time past ye walked according to the course of this world, according to the prince of the power of the air, the spirit that now worked in the children of disobedience; among whom also we all had our conversation in times past in the lusts of our flesh, fulfilling the desires of the flesh and of the mind; and were by nature the children of wrath, even as others."

The message is clear - we were not sinners by choice. We were sinners by nature! We were born into this condition, simply because the first man, Adam, put us all into slavery to sin. We had nothing to say about it. We did not in any way will it, consent to it, or choose it, for we were born into it. And we were not born free moral agents. We were born slaves!

There is no fact more self-evident than the fact of the total depravity of man, or his total inability to deliver himself from bondage to sin, and this is rooted in the fact that his human spirit is dead from birth. Total depravity means that man in his natural state is incapable of doing anything or desiring anything pleasing to God. Until our spirit is quickened by HIS SPIRIT we are slaves of the flesh and the devil and are enemies to God. When man insists that he still has a "spark" of divine good resident in his heart the Bible says, "The heart is deceitful above all things and desperately wicked. Who can know it?" (Jer. 17:9). When man contends that he is a free moral agent and can accept or reject the Lord by his own volition, the Word of God contradicts him, declaring, "There is none righteous, no not one! There is none that understandeth, there is none that seeketh after God" (Rom. 3:10-11).

Man is totally depraved in the sense that everything about his nature is in rebellion against God. Man is loyal to the god of darkness and loves darkness rather than The Light. His will is, therefore, not at all "free." It is a slave to the flesh.

Total depravity means that man, of his own free will," will never make a decision for Christ. Our blessed Lord bluntly says, "Ye will not come to me, that ye might have life" (Jn. 5:40). Why does our Lord say this? Because the will of the unregenerate man is bound by the bands of sin and death to the god of the spiritually dead.

Total depravity means that the natural man is completely incapable of discerning Truth. In fact, unregenerate man thinks of the things of God as being ridiculous! "The natural man receives not the things of the Spirit of God; for they are foolishness to him. Neither can he know them, because they are spiritually discerned" (I Cor. 2:14). Man cannot see or know the things which relate to the Kingdom of God, without being regenerated first by the Holy Spirit. A dead spirit perceives only the things of man and Satan.

Hence the words of Jesus to Nicodemus: "Unless a man is born again, he cannot see the Kingdom of God" (Jn. 3:3). Unborn children do not see the light. Dead men do not see the light. Unregenerate men cannot comprehend even that they should come to the Light. They are the unborn dead who know only darkness. They are totally depraved, wholly incapable of thinking, perceiving, or doing anything pleasing to God, until God sees fit to give them life and understanding. Faith follows the giving of Life. The giving of Life is by the will of God. Notice the order: "God, who is rich in mercy, for His great love with which He loved us, even when we were dead in sins, hath made us alive together with Christ (by grace are ye saved)" (Eph. 2:4-5). Man is not saved by some mythical act of his own free will. He is saved by grace, the divine enablement of God who first gives him Life and then imparts faith in his heart as a free gift. Paul continues: "For by grace are ye saved through faith, and that not of yourselves; it is the Gift of God. It is not of works, lest any man should boast" (Eph. 2:8-9).

Observe! Saving faith is the gift of God, not an exercise of man's free will!" Man must believe, certainly, but it is not the old deceitful and desperately wicked heart, nor the old carnal mind which believes, but the faith graciously imparted by God as a gift is the agency of man's believing. God has decreed that the works of the flesh shall have no part in the "so great salvation" which He Himself provides. It is His work through the Gift of Life.

He regenerated us when we were dead in sins. Life is His Gift. Faith is His Gift. We are saved by a faith which "is not of ourselves." We believed by the faith which GOD gives, not by our own free will! Until a man has been quickened by the Holy Spirit the word is: "Why do ye not understand my speech? Even because ye cannot hear my word! Ye are of your father the devil" (Jn. 8:43-44).

But once God quickens us by the Gift of Life and the Gift of Faith the word is: "It is God who works in you both to will and to do of His good pleasure" (Phil. 2:13).

Wise men standing by the grave of Lazarus might pronounce it an evidence of insanity when the Lord addressed a dead man with the words, "Lazarus, Come forth." Ah! But He who thus spake was and is Himself the Resurrection, and the Life, and at HIS word even the dead live!

Just as Lazarus would never have heard the voice of Jesus, nor would he have ever "come to Jesus," without first being given Life by our Lord, so all men "dead in trespasses and sins," must first be given Life by God before they can "come to Christ." Since dead men cannot will to receive Life, but can be raised from the dead only by the power of God, so the natural man cannot of his own mythical "free will," will to have eternal life (Jn. 10:26-28). He must be given God's gift of saving faith. If Jesus had had no more than an "invitation" for Lazarus to receive Life, He could have knocked at that tombstone door for a long time. But Christ spoke the Life-giving Word and that Word brought Lazarus to life and caused his heart to begin to beat and his lungs to work, and Lazarus heard the voice of his Master and received the faith to arise and walk out of the darkness of that tomb of death.

The natural man is a third rate power. He is not able to resist Satan because his will is inferior to the will of the devil. Paul says that those who oppose the ministers of God's truth are in the snare of the devil and "are taken captive by him at his will" (II Tim. 2:26). How can the devil ensnare the lost "at his will"? For the simple reason that man, without the Holy Spirit, is an inferior power who cannot resist the devil but walks "according to the course of this world, according to the Prince of the power of the air, the spirit that now worketh in the children of disobedience" (Eph. 2:2). And consequently, Jesus says, "No man can come to me, except the Father which hath sent me draw him" (Jn.6:44). A plain example of this is the business woman named Lydia who heard the apostles teaching the Word of God, and "whose heart he Lord opened... "(Acts 16:14). Who opened her heart to Jesus? Does the Bible teach that the sinner opened her heart to the Lord, or does the Scripture teach that it is the Lord who opens hearts?

As someone has said, "Here is a man that is dead, lying in a casket in the ground. What will you do to raise him? Will you bring your flute and play a sweet melody to woo him out of the grave? Perhaps a great thunderstorm could come and the lightning could strike around him and the thunder could shake the earth and boom and crash with its mighty voice.

But neither the sweet music of the flute nor the mighty thundering above would have any affect whatsoever on the dead in their graves. They hear not; neither do they know. Nor, can the thundering of the Law or the sweet music of the Gospel have any effect on the mind and soul that is dead in sin. It needs one thing. It needs to be made alive! By a power beyond itself! 'You hath He made alive that were dead.' "Therefore, until God first of all comes with His grace and make men alive, there is nothing that man can do. Only God can raise the dead! True, God requires repentance and faith that we might be saved. But, praise His name that which He requires, He also freely gives, that the whole thing may be of grace.

Yet some proclaimed Christians insists on a doctrine of man being a "free moral agent," even though the Word of God exposes this as being utterly false in every degree. Most emphatically do I declare: We are not free moral agents! "The creature was made subject to vanity, not willingly, but by reason of Him who hath subjected the same in hope" (Rom. 8:20).

Summarily, a school of thought suggests that Satan like every other human possesses a spirit of choice, to choose between good and evil. Kind begets kind; God is good {Matthew 19:17} therefore, He must have created Satan good, but Satan choose disobedience and rebellion, like every man can choose to do good or evil. (Joshua 24: 15; Isaiah 6:15-16). Do you remember that choice is the chance or ability to choose between alternatives, thus that Satan made a choice had also conformed the existence of good along side with evil because options and alternatives must exist before anyone would make a choice.

The fact that Satan made a choice had conformed that evil was really in existence alongside with its alternative, good. Even in the book of Deuteronomy 30:15, The Lord declared, See, I have set before thee this day life and good, and death and evil. Then who invented this evil! Was evil included in the perfection of God's creations? How does this thought of pride, disobedience and rebellion come to be? However, suggesting that Satan's mind invented these thoughts would directly imply that God's creation was not good and perfect.

EVIL AND THE GARDEN OF EDEN

The word evil was first mentioned in the book of Genesis 2:9 "and the Lord God planted a garden eastward in Eden; and there he put the man whom he had formed ...in the middle of the garden were the tree of life and the tree of the knowledge of good and evil.

Earth was without form and void until God created land out of waters as this was the genesis of human life. God made this garden that was inseparably associated with the theological dogma of original sin; He made the trees to grow including the tree of knowledge of good and evil. He gave the trees fertility to bear fruits including the tree of knowledge of good and evil and He put to test the freewill and destiny of Humankind, being that He knew the end from the beginning. So, why did God allow an evil tree to grow in the mist of the beautiful garden!

Why did He not cause the tree to be fruitless or does He not know that the tree of knowledge of good and evil will bring the failure of Man! Does He not know that Man will fall? Rather He commanded the man saying, you are free to eat from any tree in the garden; but you must not eat from the tree of the knowledge of good and evil, for when you eat of it you will surely die.

This clause: "when you eat of it, you will surely die" connotes assurance and certainty that God knew the effects of the tree right from the creation of the garden and thereafter, Lord God said, the man has now become like one of us, knowing good and evil. Gen 3:22-24.

THE TRUTH ABOUT EVIL

The force evil seems to be older than all creations of God, which means evil, had been in existence even before the creations of the earth. Even the presence of darkness before creation substantiates this truth as darkness is synonymous with evil. *"Now the earth was formless and empty, darkness was over the surface of the deep...."*

This evil entered into a good angel making him the first fruit of wickedness, honorably tagged as the Evil One, his existence is real, witnessed and Biblically proven within humanity. Sin was produced by the evil principle becoming active, which began with Satan who permitted evil to control and dominate his course of action. He introduced sin and evil into the world when he induced our first parents to disobey the Divine commandment. Thus, the race has come under the dominion of sin. Sin is a transgression of Law (I John 3:4). Evil is the force that propels us to sin. It is not sin until it is put to action.

Therefore, sin is evil in action, which could be visible or invisible, physical or abstract but simply signifies what we consider as bad things. *All sin is evil but not all evil is sin.* Sometimes, God uses this evil in the best way He knows in order to accomplish His purposes and for His glory. He may allow evil in order that He might display his wrath and judgment just for our reproof. As He said: "I form the light, and create darkness: I make peace, and create evil: I the Lord do all these things" (Isaiah 45:7).

See all of Isaiah 54:16 and Amos 3:6, two of the many scriptures that show how God uses evil in any way he wants. It is highly unbiblical and blasphemous to believe that both evil and a good most powerful God co-exist, digging deeper or trying to apply a logical reasoning will definitely run us into profanations as ordinary human mind cannot penetrate the source of good and evil because it is beyond the reach of human intellect.

We do invent various theories, philosophies, doctrines, and religions by which we attempt to explain and become comfortable with this fundamental mystery. Nevertheless, no matter how much we philosophize, we fail to know the deeper Divine origin of good and evil because it is a divine secret, which in this instance the intellect cannot provide. God cannot lie (Tit. 1:2). Neither can He be tempted to sin, nor can He tempt others to sin (James 1:13). In other words, He cannot do anything that will corrupt his holy nature.

The book Habakkuk Chapter 1 declared that God is of purer eyes to approve evil or behold evil. He cannot look on wickedness. 1 Corinthians 14:33 declares that God is not the author of confusion rather confusion is a product of sin. God is light, and in Him is no darkness at all.1 John 1:5

God cannot be tempted with evil, neither tempts He any man. James 1:13 All that is in the world, all evil categorically, the lust of the flesh, the lust of the eyes, the pride of life, is not of the Father. 1 John 2:16. Psalm 5:4: You are not a God who has pleasure in wickedness; neither will evil dwell with you. In fact, on a positive note, Isaiah 6 revealed the antiphonal cry of the angels that God is "Holy, holy, and holy."

There is only one evil seed, the accuser of brethren, a murderer from the beginning, not holding to the truth, for there is no truth in him, when he speaks he lies, he speaks his native language, for he is a liar and the father of lies. Since we know that God's creations were all perfectly and beautifully made, May I submit, the truth remains that there is no Biblical evidence about the origin of evil but there are things we do not know and that should be the secret things of the Almighty God as clearly stated in Deuteronomy 29 vs. 29.

The secret things belong unto the Lord our God: but those things which are revealed belong unto us. A mere contemporary and chronological gen of Satan is not sufficient to expose and resist him but a contactual and inspirational power of the almighty God through the Holy Spirit will teach and direct us the more. Ours is not to be concerned so much with what God is doing in His heart, rather the question for us is; what are we doing with our own? I advised that we should be silent where the Bible is silent.

~ 3 ~

Evil Devices

Satan often hinders the effectiveness of preaching by creating disorder in a meeting through reckless talks and questioning. He may even interrupt a sermon by stirring up a drunken man to come forward and ask for prayer

Understanding the will of God and applying the gained knowledge on a continuing basis is imperative to the growth of our daily Christian living. God's divine power has granted us all things that pertain to life and godliness, through the knowledge of Him who called us to His own glory and excellence, by which He has established us His precious and very great promises, that through these we may escape from the corruption that is in the world because of lust, and become partakers of the divine nature even His eternal promises.

For this very reason, you should make every effort to supplement your faith with virtue, and virtue with knowledge, and knowledge with self-control, and self-control with steadfastness, and steadfastness with godliness, and godliness with brotherly affection, and brotherly affection with love; but our arch enemy, Satan has his motives destructively centered on making us come short of these divine promises. Been mad at God from the very moment he was kicked out of heaven unto this earth, He redoubled his efforts to defeat the work of Christ in man's behalf and to fasten souls in his snares. To hold people in darkness and impenitence till the Savior's mediation is over, and there is no longer a sacrifice for sin.

This is just the destructive motive he seeks to accomplish. He does everything he can to disrupt the work that God loves, the work of his church, Christian families and individual Christians. When there is no special effort made to resist his power, when indifference prevails in the church and the world, Satan is not concerned; for he is in no danger of losing those whom he is leading captive at his will. But when the attention is called to eternal things, and souls are inquiring, "What must I do to be saved?" he is on the ground, seeking to match his power against the power of Christ and to counteract the influence of the Holy Spirit. This calls for serious spiritual awareness, we need to do just as our text says, being on guard every day. *II Thessalonians 2:7, Satan is already working. "For the mystery of iniquity doth already work: only he who now letteth will let, until he be taken out of the way." This can be clearly seen in Revelation 13:1-3, which describes the Anti-Christ kingdom as revealed in Daniel in the kingdoms of Babylon, Medes and Persians, Greece and Rome. The Anti-Christ kingdom develops slowly over time, and the time for the full revelation of Satan's kingdom is very near at hand.*

Satan hinders the work and word of God as was exemplarily seen in book of Daniel 10:12-13, where it was revealed that for twenty-one days an invisible battle was fought between the angel of God and the prince of darkness. God's angels are spirits; we know the prince of Persia as well cannot be a man of flesh and blood; rather, he is an evil spirit, a devil.

That means for twenty-one days Daniel's prayer had been answered but was hindered by the evil one. Therefore, for twenty-one days angel was putting devil to flight for the sake of Daniel. This book revealed to us what could possibly prevail in the realm of the spirit whenever we pray. When Abraham and Sarah had the promise of a son, both Abimelech and Pharaoh wanted Sarah to be their wife but these were men that could have anyone they wanted, then why Sarah? They would have interfered with the plan of God had not the Lord spoke and warned them not to touch Sarah.

Then when Satan wanted to destroy Joseph, he sent Potifer's wife, who couldn't get him to sin, so she falsely accused him and got him thrown into prison. Yet in it, because of His faithfulness to God, we see the promise of Romans 8:28.

When the Israelites were coming out of Egypt on the way to the Promised Land, Korah and his household rose up against Moses along with 250 princes who started a rebellion in the wilderness to stop God's purposes. Satan used this man's bad attitude to attack Moses but God stopped his plans. Look at Samson. He was doing God's will in destroying the Philistines, but when Satan wanted to disrupt his vision and calling, he sent a woman named Delilah. She did more damage to him than the 1000 Philistines he had slew with nothing but the jawbone of an ass.

David was doing great, had defeated all his enemies up to this point, including Goliath. But when Satan wanted to stop David and destroy his future and the promise of God for a kingdom for his seed and that the Messiah to come through his seed, he brought Bathsheba which cost David his sons. It wasn't the adultery that cost him his sons but the murder of Uriah to cover up his adultery. Then there was Solomon, who in the beginning had a heart for God and spent 7 years building the most fantastic temple for God, but the Bible tells us that when he was old, strange women turned his heart away from God.

More so, Lord Jesus went further to illustrate how Satan can hinder the germination of the sown word in Mark 4:15; the ones who are beside the road where the word is sown; and when they hear, immediately Satan comes and takes away the word that has been sown in them. In addition, the book of 1 Thessalonica 2:18 tell us how Paul was hindered severally in his mission. "For we wanted to come to you- I, Paul, more than once and yet Satan hindered us". Satan had tried many times to hinder Paul mission as seen in Acts 17 vs.13.

When the Jews of Thessalonica found out that Paul in Berea had proclaimed the word of God also, they came there as well, agitating and stirring up the crowds. Nevertheless, it will really be wonderful seeing the work of God growing and prospering, but Satan is doing all he can to stop it and causing his work to increase. He puts heated discussion between couples so that their prayers will be hindered as seen in I Peter 3:7. He might cause two brethren to fall out over some minor issues just to hinder the work of the Lord. Satan puts on a big campaign to control people's emotions.

Emotionalism can lead to great distractions for Christians, though emotion is a bona fide function of the soul, whenever it takes precedence over Bible truth, it leads to distraction. Those who dabble in ecstatic experiences, public or private, are allowing their feelings and emotions to outweigh doctrine. Satan also promotes heavily in the area of mental attitude sins such as fear, worry, bitterness, desires for revenge, pride, guilt feelings, lack of love, failure to forgive, hatred, mental adultery, and so forth. The mental attitude sin is the worst category because it is so devastating, for as long as it takes place, the Word of God is being ignored.

Satan's sophisticated device ranges from causing a baby to cry in church so that the mother will not digest sermons to providing your immediate desire so that you will be carried away by lust. There are more biblical examples of where Satan tried to hinder the work of God:

a. When Ezra and Nehemiah restored the wall and temple of Jerusalem, there were always those mockers, who did everything they could do to hinder the work. There were particularly three enemies: Sanballat, Tobiah and Geshem, plus a whole crowd of people that gathered together in an external sense to oppose the work of God that Nehemiah was doing. Read Nehemiah 4 and 6. In recent times, there are also members of the church who mocks and despises church builders. These mockers will not build also will prevent willful members from building. They will not donate but will like to know the highest donor and the total amount donated.

b. Joshua led the Israelites to capture the cities of Canaan, but Satan hindered by coaxing Achan to disobey the clear commands of God, causing Israel to be defeated at Ai. Achan's disobedience infected the Israelites campaign to take the city of Ai. Instead of victoriously conquering Ai, thirty-six Israelites were killed and the Israelites ran from the people of Ai in defeat. Next time you think about disobeying God, consider who may suffer the consequences of your disobedience. If you choose to disobey God, you may destroy someone, something or be hindering the work of God. Read Joshua 7.

c. When Moses stood before Pharaoh and cast down his rod, which became a serpent, Satan hindered by causing the magicians of Egypt to cast down their rods, which also became serpents. The story did not end until the serpents of God ate up the serpents of the magicians. This signifies how he often hinders the true gospel by sending impostors, the likes of the truth to preach another gospel.

d. Satan hinders Christians when they are earnest in prayer by creating all forms of distractions and unsettle mindedness. He also could stir us to work when we should be in prayer; or interrupt prayer by sending someone in; the doorbell or phone bell may ring. Sometimes he may send direct opposition like tiredness and drowsiness so that it is difficult to pray.

e. A Christian may be hindered in money matters by these evil spirits detaining, or turning aside business or money that is needed for personal needs or for God's works. You may have experienced this as well, even the Church sometimes become broke. Satan distracts by trying to keep believers from public assembly worship, Heb. 10:25. He tempts the believer with an improper emphasis on details of life such as money, success, social life, pleasure, loved ones, health, sex, materialistic things, or status symbols. The mature believer knows that his happiness is not derived from these things, so he is not a slave to them. The novice Christian, however, may try to gain happiness from such things, and this will distract him from the Word of God.

f. Satan also hinders the effectiveness of preaching by creating disorder in a meeting through careless or reckless talks and questioning. He may even interrupt a sermon by stirring up a drunken man to come forward and ask for prayer. The preaching stopped in order to try to help the supposed penitent, but he received nothing and the meeting was hindered for that moment.I have also witnessed a revival meeting where electricity unexpectedly went off and the Church generating set refused turning on just at the middle of the night.

g. Satan sometimes stirs people up against a servant of God to try to break him down. These may be in form of accusation, gossip or unreasonable argument about the scripture. Another of his wiles is to get a hearer to criticize the preacher's manner, appearance, or speech instead of listening fairly to what he has to say. Or they may get the preacher into a hard, abusive, impatient method, or into extreme statements. And they get people to eyeing and criticizing each other, and so hinder them from receiving God's blessing. A spiritual work was once almost entirely ruined because the people in it were deceived into "discerning" each other's condition.

Satan work on people's fear or prejudices to keep them from getting the benefit of God's truth or he may misrepresent the truth. How many people have a wrong view of the teaching of those who uphold the truth of sanctification by faith! These spirits stir people to bigotry, intolerance and persecution, so that they think everyone not in this movement is on the way to hell, and they say so.

Many believers still coddle offenses and grudges as though they were "pets" to be fed and watered. Unforgiveness is one of

Satan's devices, an instrument, a weapon, a plot, a scheme, and a tool, that he uses to devastate the church of Christ, destroy family and ruin lives forever. People that Satan could not get to rob a bank or shoot someone; he gets to them through strife, bitterness, resentment and unforgiveness; things that many people wouldn't describe as awful sin. Paul said "forgive, lest Satan should get an advantage of us"; That tells us that unforgiveness in our heart can give Satan an advantage over us, a way of controlling us, robbing us of our joy, our deliverance, our peace, our love, harmony in the home, the victory of overcoming, from possessing all of the promises of God, our prosperity and our salvation

Unforgiveness stops God's harvest in your life and your prayers from being answered. It defiles a Christian as declared the book of Hebrews 12:15, "...lest any root of bitterness springing up trouble you, and thereby many are defiled." Is it really possible to lose one's salvation by merely holding a grudge against someone? Jesus left no room for doubt on the subject. He clearly stated that we cannot have God's forgiveness if we choose to withhold forgiveness toward others. "For if you forgive men their trespasses, your heavenly Father will also forgive you. But if you do not forgive men their trespasses, neither will your Father forgive your trespasses" (Matt 6:14-15). It's no wonder why Satan works so hard to stir up turmoil, and tries to keep us from forgiving and loving each other. If he can deceive us into harboring bitterness, he knows that we will exempt ourselves from God's forgiveness of our sins, and will ultimately go to the lake of fire (Rev. 20:15). The consequences of unforgiveness are reiterated in many scriptures: Matt. 18:21-35, Mark 11:25-26, Matt. 6:12, Luke 6:37, Luke 11:4.

Unforgiveness is so dangerous that if you are walking therein, Satan is not obligated to listen to your rebuke. Mark 11:25 *"And when ye stand praying, forgive, if ye have ought against any: that your Father also which is in heaven may forgive you your trespasses."* Matthew 5:23-24 *"Therefore if thou bring thy gift to the altar, and there rememberest that thy brother hath ought against thee; Leave there thy gift before the altar, and go thy way; first be reconciled to thy brother, and then come and offer thy gift.*" Don't even bother to give a gift to the Lord if you have unforgiveness in your heart because if you do, God won't receive it. Isaiah 59:2-3 said *"But your iniquities have separated between you and your God, and your sins have hid his face from you that he will not hear. For your hands are defiled with blood, and your fingers with iniquity; your lips have spoken lies, your tongue hath muttered perverseness."*

If God doesn't hear our prayer because of sin, then what makes you think Satan will listen to you? You will become like sounding brass and a tinkling symbol. 1 Corinthians 13:1 *"Though I speak with the tongues of men and of angels, and have not charity, I am become as sounding brass, or a tinkling cymbal."* Your words will be nothing but noise if you have not love.

Sometimes, a Christian might see temptation as opportunity because Satan makes evil appear good. His tricks may come in the form of a valuable gift or a lucrative offer, just like the case of Joseph; sleeping with Potiphar's wife would have brought a temporary promotion but definitely death because the same demon that induced her into seducing Joseph would also gossip to Potiphar about his wife's unfaithfulness. He does not appear as though he is the destruction of men, if he appears like a red creature with horns and a pitchfork, with the smell of brimstone on him, nobody would follow him.

The apostle Paul warns against false prophets and false teachers who in the name God propagates evil, they do not tell the truth nor warn you of the consequences of sin, but try to say that everything is relevant, that it is sin only if we think it is sin; preaching prosperity even to a sinful believer. Satan never shows the true consequences of sin and rebellion against God, but always shows the pleasures of sin. Unconsciously a Christian may lend himself to demons to be used against another Christian.

h. Finally, he can hinder the call of God in you by cursing your business to prosper uncommonly. An excessive in-flow of money and connections will definitely make some believers settle the world rather than the word. Beware, one of Satan's tricks is to give you a better job that will pull you away from the place God has called you to be. It will pull you away from the Bible studies God wants you to partake of. It will pull you away from the church God wants you to go to, and from works God has called you to do. Many of these things may come upon you; therefore beware of the deceitfulness of riches. It seems much of the advertising around us is centered on getting, keeping, maintaining, insuring, and loving the things of this world. Thus, much of what we see and hear tends to pull us in the opposite direction that God would have us go.

Beware of Satan and his cunning devices. Beware, lest the world pulls you in like a magnet, and you cannot get free. Put all your trust in Christ and get rid of those things which hinder you from following Jesus totally. Paul tells us what our attitude should be, I count all things but loss for the excellence of the knowledge of Christ Jesus; for whom I have suffered the loss of all things and do count them but dung that I may win Christ. - Philippians 3:8.

A saved person should esteem the reproach of Christ greater riches than all the riches of this world. Thus, by faith the born-again Christian should forsake this world, and live for the world to come. Love not this world, or the things that are in this world. Read: Matt. 13:39; Mark 4:15; 2 Cor. 11:14, 15; 2 Thess. 2:9, 10; Rev. 2:10; 3:9.

DEVIL HINDERS CONVERSION

The devil is very busy preventing people from receiving Christ. He hardens the hearts of unbelievers, made them blind to gospel by exercising negative volition toward the Word of God. He does not force anyone to be lost but uses every means to scare the unbeliever away from the truth. His ultimate weapons in these are religion and humanism. He tries to promote the glorification and deification of mankind while downgrading God In Luke 8:11 Christ Jesus illustrated the parable of sower, verse 12 says, those by the wayside are they that hear; then cometh the devil, and taketh away the word out of their hearts, lest they should believe and be saved. Verse 5 tells us that the wayside seed was trodden down.

The path was rock hard, so when the seed fell on it, it remained on the surface and birds ate it. When people with hard hearts hear God's Word, they do not receive it then comes the devil and takes it away. Our situations determines how the word will be received, when the Word of God lands on a heart that is indifferent, callous, and unresponsive, the devil snatches it away. Second Corinthians 4:3-4 says, "If our gospel be hidden it is hidden to them that are lost, in whom the god of this age [Satan] hath blinded the minds of them who believe not. Satan blinds the minds of those who willfully disbelieve God. It does mean that Satan can make a person blind to spiritual truth because such person has an unbelieving heart to begin with. To people with hard hearts the gospel is irrelevant. As 1 Corinthians 1 verses 18 rightly said, the preaching of the cross is to them that perish foolishness. The devil is the author of spiritual blindness.

We can conquer Satan through the blood of Jesus and the word of our testimony. See John 8:44; 12:37-40; Acts 26:18; 2 Corinthians 4:4 and 2 Timothy 2:26. Are you irregular in church services, do you lack interest in worship and bible classes, do you consistently arrive late to services, are you waning efforts to win souls for Christ, do you feel tired having your private devotion? Any 'yes' to the above questions signifies a spiritual problem.

SUBTLE AND CUNNING

Picture a man who suddenly leaps in front of you without warning from a dark alley. He has a machine gun in his hands, ammunition belts over his shoulders, a crazed look of insanity in his eye and anger is written on his brow. Then picture another man who is gentle. His words are kind. He is well-dressed and peaceful.

You have known him all your life. There is nothing about him to arouse suspicion. But unknown to you, that man is secretly plotting your assassination. He carries in his pocket a vial of arsenic with which he has been secretly poisoning your food and water, a little at a time, for years. Which of these two men is more frightening?

Obviously, the first one. Which of the two is more dangerous? Without question, the second! The first man frightens you, because he appears suddenly with the obvious intent to do you harm. But when he appears, you immediately prepare to defend yourself. The second man does not scare you at all. You think he is a friend. He is a frequent guest in your home. You feel no need to defend yourself from him. But he is gradually, subtly killing you. And you are totally unaware of it. That makes Satan far more dangerous. Genesis 3:1-6; Matthew 4; Luke 4; 2 Corinthians 11:3, 14; Rev 12:9.

DECEPTIONS AND SEDUCTION

The increase of evil in the world is the result of satanic deception of the nations. The leaders and citizenry are lost because Satan has blinded the eyes of them all from seeing the light. His major weapons are unconcealed falsehood, innuendo, insinuation and doubt. His first attack on mankind was to plant a seed of doubt in Eve's mind which was the genesis of our problems today. Relentlessly, he is still in the business of planting same seed in the mind of men. This is why he has convinced many that he does not exist. John 8:44 and Isaiah 14: 13-14. He sows tares among the wheat-Matthew 24:30. He sows false doctrine - 1 Timothy 4:1-3. He defiles the Word of God by

a. **Taking it out of context** - In order to sustain erroneous doctrines or unchristian practices, Satan sometimes will seize upon passages of Scripture separated from the context, perhaps quoting half of a single verse as proving their point, when the remaining portion would show the meaning to be quite the opposite. Matthew 4:6 - In this passage, he quoted Psalm 91:11 but conveniently left out the part "To keep thee in all thy ways."

b. **Misinterpretation of the word.**

c. **Overstressing one-sided doctrine.**

d. **Under stressing certain doctrines like the doctrine of Satan.**

e. **Causing people to put a meaning into Scripture that is not there.**

Satan works among his own people by influencing governments and nations. When he was unmasked in Isaiah 14 and Ezekiel 28, on both occasions the prophets were speaking to a human ruler but they were actually addressing Satan, who was influencing those rulers. Also Daniel 10:13, 20 referred to certain nations that were governed by men possessed by demons. Satan has always been active in politics. When he tempted our Lord in Matthew 4:1-11, he offered Christ the kingdoms of the world if He would bow down to him (vv. 8-9). Although Satan is a usurper, as prince of this world he does indeed hold sway over the kingdoms of the world.

In this age Satan and demons are desperate to buy you, they weren't there when God designed you but they are now knocking incessantly at your door to know if you can compromise your faith. They often appear like answers from above but do not be deceived for Satan himself is transformed into an angel of light. He never presents sin as it really is. He never presents both sides of the story, pro and con. He presents only what he wants us to see, something that appears fun and exciting. He wants us to focus on pleasure, on what feels or looks good at the moment. He wants long-term consequences to be the last thing on our minds while he entices us to sin. He knew you are facing a serious problem and want to tempt you at the very point of need. All he wants is to estrange you with God and rob you off your divine rights.

What are your Divine rights?

That you will flourish like the palm tree and grow like a cedar in Lebanon. You shall be like a tree planted by the rivers of water that bringeth forth his fruit in his season; his leaf also shall not wither; and whatsoever you doeth shall prosper. You are like a green olive tree in the house of God, your branches shall spread, and your beauty shall be as the olive tree, and your smell as Lebanon. Psalm 92:12, Psalm 1:3, and Psalm 52:8 and Hosea14:6. The rights to ask seek and knock, for this is the confidence that you (Christians) have before Him (God), that, if you ask anything according to His will, He hears you. You are also equipped with sophisticated anti-satanic gadgets as God declares that no weapon that is formed against you will prosper; and every tongue that accuses you in judgment you will condemn. This is the heritage of the servants of the Lord, their vindication is from," declares the Lord.

These are your wonderful birthrights; heavenly instituted privileges that offer a fulfilled Christian living but the devil want to steal these rights from you. You are a house Of God, 2 Corinthians 5 vs. 1 declares you are a house wonderfully and beautifully designed by God. This is why God have decided to live in you. You are the temple of the Holy Ghost, Jesus said if you will open your heart, my father and I will come and make our abode in you, meaning that you should be a sanctified house. You ought to offer your body as a living sacrifice unto God. Your body is a place where God should dwell. It is the anointed abode where the glory of God should be seen, dedicated for Holy purposes. But Satan often manipulates the mind of Christians, setting up confusion and indecisiveness; justifying lies and making wrong look right.

He can easily seduce a wayward Christian by placing a valuable offer, an offer that may not easily be refused by a mere man. He often could disguise a pitiful appearance; only trying to gain your attention. This is his seduction scheme, the brain behind fashion these days. What is the intention for dressing naked to the waist? What is the intention for exposing your womanhood? What is the intention for putting half skirt or wearing a dress that transmits your body shape? All these intentions are just to create a lustful attention. Will you be happy enjoying your display as you brother dies in lust? Lust is a demon-spirit that turns the natural drive of reproduction into unnatural sexual expression. See 1 Chronicles 21:1; John 13:2, 27; Acts 5:3.

AFFLICTING PHYSICAL AND SPIRITUAL ILLNESS ON HUMANKIND

Job 1, Matt 9:32-33, 12:22; Mk 1:26; 9:17-25; Judges 9:23, 1 Sam 16:14; 18:9-11; 19:9;2 Chronicles 18:20-22; Matt 4:24, 17:15, Mk 5:5, 15, 18; 9:22; Luke 8:27, 35, 36.

Just as Satan did to Job, He believes that afflicting us with illness will force us to deny God. He uses sickness to shake our faith in God, scatter the confidence and possibly ruin our spirit being. He does often just to pollute the peace and joy we have in the Lord, even in the sickness; he brings the fear of death.

There is a faithful consolation, though he may afflicts us with illness, in Christ we have spiritual life that is focused on giving glory to God, serving Christ in joy knowing that we who are in this tent groan, being burdened, not because we want to be unclothed, but further clothed, that mortality may be swallowed up by life. For we know that if our earthly house, this tent, is destroyed, we have a building from God, a house not made with hands, eternal in the heavens. 2 Corinthians. 5:1 and 4.

GATHERING MORE SOULS FOR HELL AND HADES

This is Satan main objective for deceiving and hindering word. He wants the world to partake in his eternal condemnation but God forbid! He shall ever be in hell as the one who inflicts torment on others. He will be cast into hell to be tormented, though he now inhabits the heavenly realms (Eph. 6 vs.12), has access to God (Job 1:6), and is active upon the earth (Job 1:7; 1 Pet. 5:8), but finally Satan will be cast into hell. We have already noted that hell has been prepared for him and his angels.

In the following Scripture we have the accounts of how he will be cast into hell: "And the devil that deceived them was cast into the lake of fire and brimstone, where are also the beast and the false prophet; and they shall be tormented day and night for ever and ever" (Rev. 20:10). This is to take place at the end of the "little season" during which Satan is to be loosed again after the millennium. The beast and the false prophet are to be cast into the lake of fire preceding the millennium (Rev. 19:20).

The Bible talks of hell as a place of torment where a sinner goes after death while waiting for the final judgment. All who did not receive Jesus Christ as their Lord and Savior, shall be in hell when they die. For this main reason, Satan is working tirelessly to propagate the gate of hell. We can only avoid hell when we refuse to yield to his devices. The Bible has clearly warned us about hell in the following verses: But I say unto you, whosoever shall say, thou fool, shall be in danger of hell fire Matt 5:22. The wicked shall be turned into hell and all the nations that forget God Psalms 9:17-18. Please see Mark 9:43, Matthew 3:10; Isaiah 14:12; Zech 3:1-2; and Ezekiel 28:17.

In line with trying to prevent our abundant life in Christ Jesus, the devil tries steals our peace by making us anxious, worried, and troubled. He knows that when our joy is gone, we are automatically made weak in the spirit, giving to thinking and overshadowed by worries. When our joy is gone, we rarely pray, we cannot read the Bible nor witness to sinners. When our joy is gone, we advertise our problems instead of petitioning God. When our joy is gone, we are faithless; without faith, it is impossible to please God (Hebrews 11:6) and if faith is stolen from us, we turn away from the Lord. When our joy is gone, we settle for the less. When our joy is gone, we might even go for divination. Let me illustrate this with a true-life story. In city center of Bende lived a happy but poor couple. Regardless of their childlessness and poverty, they were joyous daily, singing praise to God every moment. They read their bible together, joyfully sharing any inspiration revealed.

But one day the cunning serpent crept into the heart of a rich neighbor of theirs, who offered to help them start up business just to alleviate their poverty and to help them make a better living. I believe this offering was of the devil, an offering from the Greece to Troy. They accepted the offer and went into business but this automatically took their joy away. They now settled for counting money, keeping and updating business records. There was no time for singing and praying as they usually do; their life became a bit comfortable.

One day the Holy Spirit revealed their situation to the wife in a dream, she then realized that the money was an offering from an occultist whom their prayers and praise have been troubling. To cut the story short, they returned the money and gained back their joy in the Lord. This is just how Satan uses your immediate desire to entice you. He appears like bringing a solution but actually intends destroying you. Thank God for the Holy Spirit.

SELF AMBITIOUS AND STRONG WILL

Isaiah 14:12-15; Ezekiel 28:17. Isaiah pointed out five "I will" that came out from the proud and boastful heart of Satan which described the nature of his aspiration (Isaiah. 14:13-14).

- I will ascend to heaven.
- I will raise my throne above the stars of God.
- I will sit on the mount of the assembly in the recesses of the north.
- I will ascend above the heights of the clouds.
- I will make myself like the Most High

He had a strong will to achieve these objectives but God prevailed. Even to this day, no matter how many times you cast out a demon, he will always want to recoup his previous abode. Everyday, Satan is being defeated in the life of many Christian worldwide but he never give up, he fights tirelessly to achieve his aim. If all Christians should be as tireless as Satan in our prayers and supplication, the gate of hell will not have any soul.

Cursed and Humiliated

In Genesis 3 vs. 14, the LORD God said unto the serpent, because thou hast done this, thou art cursed above all cattle, and above every beast of the field... Upon thy belly, thou shalt go: and dust shalt thou eat all the days of thy life. He is not eternal, not omniscient, not omnipresent and not omnipotent. Luke 22:3; John 13:27; Job 1:12; 2:6 Mark 10: 34

His Imprisonment shall be in the Bottomless Pit

When Jesus Christ returns to earth Satan will be imprisoned in the bottomless pit, held there during the millennium reign of peace. After the millennium, Satan will be released from the bottomless pit. He will then go forth on his final spree of deception. He will convince the unbelieving host (resurrected at that second resurrection) that he was the one who brought them back to life. Having believed Satan all their lives, they will again believe his word and join him in an all out battle against God and His people. This futile attempt will end with Satan and his followers being cast into the lake of fire! Revelation 20

1: And I saw an angel come down from heaven, having the key of the bottomless pit, and a great chain in his hand. 2: And he laid hold on the dragon that old serpent, which is the Devil and Satan, and bound him a thousand years. 3: And cast him into the bottomless pit, and shut him up and set a seal upon him that he should deceive the nations no more, till the thousand years be fulfilled: and after that he must be loosed for a little season. 7: And when the thousand years are expired, Satan shall be loosed from his prison. 8: And shall go out to deceive the nations which are in the four quarters of the earth, Gog and

Magog, to gather them to battle: the number of whom is as the sand of the sea. 9: And they went up on the breadth of the earth, and compassed the camp of the saints about, and the beloved city: and fire came down from God out of heaven and devoured them. 10: And the Devil that deceived them was cast into the lake of fire, where the beast and the false prophet are, and shall be tormented day and night forever and ever. He is the arch-enemy and father of all liars having different names in different places which includes:

Angel of Light: Satan is a master of misrepresentation. He is the world's greatest advertiser, packaging his product so it seems attractive and appealing while in reality it is deadly poison. He wants his clients to see him as good, beneficent and trustworthy. He wants his product -sin and rejection of God-to appear enticing and inviting, and he is usually quite successful. Satan himself is transformed into an angel of light through the performances of diabolical signs and wonders in many churches of the world, thereby deceiving many.11 Corinthians 13-15.

A roaring Lion: When a lion attacks his prey he does not first roar and give his presence away. He stalks his prey because he is hungry and in need of food. Many times the female lions in the pride will work together to bring down their prey and then will allow the male that protects their pride to eat first. The pride of female lions move in silence trying to stalk their prey when they are the most defenseless. They choose the unwatched youngster or the old and weak for there victims. Satan is the same way. He does not alert the child of God first to let them know that he is up to no good. He watches for the time that a Christian is less defensive so the Christian will not have time to prepare and put his armor on. A Christian **must** at all times be prepared by keeping his or her armor on, so the enemy will not have a chance to destroy them. After Satan leads a person into sin he then roars because the child of God already knows that he has been deceived. Your adversary the devil as a roaring lion walks about seeking whom he may devour"...1 Peter 5:8.

Murderer or Liar: Satan was a murderer from the beginning and abode not in the truth, John 8:44. In that most amazing scrutiny, the Lord unfolded the devil of his disguises and revealed his true character -- a liar and a murderer. What the devil does is because of who he is, just as what we do is precisely due to what we are. Because he is a liar and a murderer, the devil's work is to deceive and to destroy. There you have the explanation for all that has been going on in human history throughout the whole course of the record of man.

Lucifer: To find the origin of Lucifer, we turn to the Old Testament. In the Hebrew, the name Lucifer is translated from the Hebrew word "helel," which means brightness. This designation, referring to Lucifer, is the rendering of the "morning star" or "star of the morning" or "bright star" which is presented in Isaiah. "How you are fallen from heaven, O Day Star, son of Dawn! How you are cut down to the ground, you who laid the nations low! You said in your heart, 'I will ascend to heaven; I will raise my throne above the stars of God; I will sit on the mount of assembly on the heights of Zaphon; I will ascend to the tops of the clouds, I will make myself like the Most High'" (Isaiah 14:12-14, NIV). The context of this passage is a referral to the king of Babylon as presented in his pride, splendor and fall. However, it is to the power behind the evil Babylonian king that this is actually addressed. No mortal king would claim that his throne was above that of God or that he was like the Most High. The power behind the evil Babylonian king is Lucifer, Son of the Morning.

The god of this world: The world listens to him, to everything he says. But the devil does not tell the world the truth but a lie, a very clever, beautiful, attractive lie which makes the world drool with desire. But the end of his lie is destruction, murder, death! -- Death in all its forms, not only ultimately the cessation of life, but also death in its incipient forms of restlessness, boredom, frustration, meaninglessness, and emptiness. Who the devil cannot deceive, he tries to destroy and whom he cannot destroy he attempts to deceive.11 Corinth 4:4: In whom the god of this world has blinded the minds of them which believe not, lest the light of the glorious gospel of Christ, who is the image of God, should shine to them.

Satan: This name of the Evil One is found over fifty-two times in the Scriptures, and it means an adversary, enemy or hater of God. Because he is the Evil One, he is the adversary of God, His ways, His works and His people, and indeed, of all people. 1 Chronicles 21:1 shows an example of his adversarial stance against the people of God: And Satan stood up against Israel, and moved David to number Israel. He hates both God and God's people. Job 1:6; 2:1; Zech 3: 1; Matt 4:10; Rev 12:9.

Devil: This name appeared 35 times in the New Testament of the Bible. It was derived from the Greek word diabolos which means slanderer and accuser. Devil means Accuser or Slanderer, and declares the chief way he seeks to cause division between God and His people, and between God's people. Matt 4:1; 13:39; Eph 4:27; Rev 12:9; 20:12.

Belial: Belial is found in 2 Corinthians 6:15, and it means worthlessness. It describes Satan's net value in God's eyes in terms of his ability to be or do anything good. Nevertheless, Scripture reveals that he, as well as the other demons, are worthy of respect, even as criminals about to be executed are normally handled with dignity in countries having a biblical heritage. Note Jude 1:8-9: 8. Yet in like manner these dreamers [false and immoral teachers] also defile the flesh, despise authority, and bring a railing accusation against [angelic] dignities. 9. But Michael the archangel, when disputing with the devil over the body of Moses, did not dare to bring a railing accusation against him, but said, The Lord rebuke thee. Similarly, 2 Peter 2:10b: They are presumptuous, self-willed, not trembling when they speak evil of angelic glories.

Anointed Cherub: This name indicates that he had one of the highest ranks of all the angels. Ezekiel 28:14.

The Prince of Power of the Air: Satan is also called the Prince of the Power of the Air - Eph. 2:2a.Though the word ''power' is singular, many commentaries believe it refers to the demonic forces as a corporate body, all of whom operate as one organized body under Satan, their ruler - Eph 6:12. This name signifies his present abode and air operations God of This Age 2 Corinthians 4:4

Ruler of Demons: Matt; 12:24; Mark 9: 34; Luke11: 15

The Wicked One: Matt 13:19, 38; 1John 2:13, 14; 3:12; 5:18

Prince of This World: Now is the time for judgment on this world; now the prince of this world will be driven out. John 12:31; 14:30; 16:11; Eph 2:1

Abaddon or Apollyon: These words means destroyer as written in Revelation 9:11. And they had a king over them which is the angel of the bottomless pit, whose name in the Hebrew tongue is Abaddon but in the Greek tongue hath his name Apollygon" In Hebrew tongues, this names signifies destruction which also had occurred in the book of Job 26:6; Proverbs 15:11.Abaddon could be seem as a place of destruction, abyss of the dead ...Job 26:6 and Proverbs 15:11.The word could also Signifies ruin and destruction. This word occurred in line with Sheol.

Evil One: Satan is the source of evil. Mark 1:13; Luke 22:3; Acts 5:3; 2 Cor. 11:14; 1 Tim. 5:15. Matt 13:19, 38. John 17:15. Eph 6: 16. The book of 1 John 5:18, 19 describe him as the personification of evil.

Beelzebub or Baalzebub: In ancient Palestine, Beelzebub means the patron god identified with the god of Ekron, Baalzebub. He is the prince of evil spirits. He is known as the "lord of the flies"... Matt 12:24, 27. Mark 3:22.LK 11:15.

Serpent: Gen 3:1. Rev 12:9. As sheep symbolizes believers, pigs for unbelievers, wolves for ferocious human so is snake a universal symbol of Satan. Satan is depicted as a serpent in about ten places in the Bible, most notably in Genesis 3:1, the first reference to him in Scripture. This depiction brings to mind his cleverness and cunning in deception, as in his temptation of Eve: Now the serpent was more cunning than any beast of the field which Jehovah God had made.

Red Dragon: Satan is portrayed as a dragon in Revelation 12, emphasizing the great power and ferocity he employed in his attempt to devour the Child of the woman (Revelation 12:4; Matthew 2), and will employ to destroy the woman, Israel, who gave birth to the Child (Revelation 12:13). Rev 12:3, 7. Dan 10:13

The Deceiver: This designation is found in Revelation 12:9, in which Satan is called, the deceiver of the whole world, showing him as the one who, by deception, deceives the great mass of humanity into rejecting God and His ways. As often as he is able he even deceives believers into rejecting God's good counsel, which is why Ephesians 6:11 exhorts us to stand against the wiles of the devil.

Adversary: An adversary is someone who stands in opposition to you or your plans. Even if an adversary cannot stop your plans, he will derive great pleasure in causing a hindrance to your work. Job 1:6-7. 9-12. 1-Peter 5:8.

The Tempter: Found in Matthew 4:3 and 1 Thessalonians 3:5, this designation shows Satan as the one who entices people to sin.

Matthew 4:3: And when the tempter came to him, he said, if thou be the Son of God, command that these stones be made bread. Matt 4:3. 1 Thessalonians 3:5

Moloch: This name was a derivation of the fire god whom children were sacrificed to. It is refers to as the abomination of the children of Anmon 1 King11: 7.Lev 18:21.20:2-5. 11 King 23:10. Jeremiah 32:35. Amos 5:26 and Acts 7:43. Satan's army is tirelessly at spiritual war against us; desperately seeking to devour and ruin our eternal hope.1 Peter 5:8.

His Armies includes:

- Demons
- Church of Satan
- Human spirits, witches, wizards and warlords
- Werewolves, werbeast and Vampires.
- Familiar Spirits
- Guiding Spirits
- Spells, Incantations, Hexes and Curses
- Marks and Hag stones.
- Songs and Movies.
- Fashions and Technologies.

~ 4 ~

THE EVIL SPIRIT FROM GOD

The nature of God is such that He never would do anything that is out of harmony with His divine Holiness. Being infinite in all His attributes including goodness and compassion, He never would mistreat anyone, manifest partiality or do something that may be legitimately indicted as wrong {Genesis 18:25}. This explanation is simple, knowing fully well that darkness or sin cannot be found in God as in 1 John 1:5,that God cannot tempt us with evil according to James 1:13-14 and He is not willing for anyone to be lost John 3:16;2 Peter 3:9. It could be unbiblical that an evil spirit will come from such a righteous God as a layman may view it. God is a multifaceted God whose thoughts are much higher than men Isaiah 55:8-9,ways are beyond tracing out Romans 11:33-36 and whose wisdom we cannot attain Psalms 139:1-6. It would not be wise if we question God's decision because He does as He wishes knowing the best for us.

That He chose Jacob over Esau does not imply He is unrighteous, or hardening Pharaoh's heart does not mean that He is wicked but what are sometimes construe as evil is simply God's punishment and reward for disobedience. In the book of Deuteronomy 28:1-14 promised were made to the Israelite if they will obey the commandments of God, in the same Deuteronomy 28:22, 25 and 29 curses were proclaimed for every disobedience.

God is the Rock on which every righteousness is founded, His work is perfect; for all His ways are just, a God of truth and without injustice; righteous and upright is He" Deuteronomy 32:4. But how can God use the devil and evil spirits to do His bidding? The bible clearly tells us that God is the cause of death. In Deuteronomy 32:39, He declares," I kill, and I make alive."Hannah, in her prayer of praise, said, "The Lord killeth, and maketh alive: He bringeth down to the grave, and bringeth up" 1 Samuel 2:6. The book Exodus 12:23 tell us concerning the first Passover, for the Lord will pass through to smite the Egyptians." Certainly, God is in charge of taking life.

However, on the other hand, the book of Hebrew 2:14 tells that Christ came to die on the cross that He might "destroy him that had the power of death that is devil." The next verse says that the devil holds the lost in bondage through the fear of death. Thus, the problem is clear for if God is in charge of death, how can the devil have the power of death? This answer explains a lot about how God uses the world of the wicked to do His bidding. The devil by nature is a murderer {John 8:44}. His rebellion against God changed his character and has made him a force that naturally kills and destroys all that comes under his power. In Revelation 9:11, he is called Abaddon and Apollyon, which means Destroyer. Paul on the other hand understands that someone may be delivered unto Satan for the destruction of the flesh. {1 Corinthians 5:5}.

This demon is called 'an evil spirit from God, because God had sent it as a punishment. God has a punitive purpose in granting this permission as He uses evil to chastise evil. More so, the term for 'evil' is a broad term that need not be referred to spiritual wickedness alone but also as physical harm or painful hardship {Genesis 19:19; 2 Samuel 17:14}. The Lord God created all things, not only the physical universe and all in it but even the heavenly beings, the angelic spirits, so by divine right He owns absolutely everything. He owns even the angels. That means he owns, even

Satan and all those who along with him rebelled against the creator and continually vie against Him.

We must understand that God is not the source of wickedness, the evil created in Isaiah 45:7 refers to bad things like earthquakes and floods, not to sin or wicked acts but He often uses the wicked to perform His own purpose. Psalm 76:10 states, "Surely the wrath of man shall praise thee: the remainder of wrath shalt thou restrain." Here we learn that God will take man's wrath toward Him and turn it into praise. There are five major occasions where God sent an evil spirit to men of disobedience.

God did send an evil spirit to Abimelech in Judges 9:23. Abimelech was a son of 70 sons Gideon or Jerubbaal, one of the leading judges of Israel, but when Gideon died, in order to prevent competition about who shall be the successor. Abimelech made a covenant with the men of Shechem and slay his 70 brothers so He could stand unopposed thereafter he was made King of Israel. Then God sent an evil spirit between Abimelech and the men of Shechem; and the men of Shechem dealt treacherously with Abimelech God repaid his wickedness by sending this evil spirit or demon to cause strive between them and this led to the death of Abimelech and many men of Shechem.

He sent this evil spirit to do his bidding which was very destructive as it was a deserved punishment for the evil committed by Abimelech and the men of Shechem. In 1 Kings 22:22 and 2 Chronicles 18:22 the Bible recorded that God sent a lying spirit in the tongues of Ahab's prophets deceiving Him to war against Ramoth Gilead so that he would be killed. Ahab's trip to Ramothgilead was his day of evil and he died because he listened to his prophets whom God, through evil spirits had deceived and as a recompense for all the evil he committed against God. This same spirit is deceiving many Christians today with fake miracles and signs leading many into hell and doing the will of devil.

In second Thessalonians 2:11 God promise to send unto those who refused to believe the truth, strong delusion. In Psalm 78:49, God judged Israel "by sending evil angels among them." And in I Samuel 16:14 God sent an evil spirit to Saul. The Bible declared that an evil spirit from God tormented Saul. However, this torment by an evil spirit did not just come without a cause. He disobeyed God in several occasion; Saul defected and David was anointed to be the next king. So, David became a conspicuous target whom Satan would want to destroy in order to discredit GOD.

It appears to me that one of Satan's fellow demons took on the task and used delinquent Saul for the job. Notice how, apparently coincidentally, David was chosen to console Saul and so David was brought into close contact with the man who quickly and unreasonably became his arch enemy. More so, Saul was rejected by God for these reasons: Instead of waiting for Samuel to arrive and offer a sacrifice before a battle, Saul offered the sacrifice himself (1 Sam. 13:8-15) - as king Saul probably believed he was a priest or at least head of the cult as was the case in other nations. Saul jeopardized the life of his son Jonathan; a favorite of the people by making a vow that Jonathan was unaware of (1 Sam. 14:1-52)

Saul did not enforce the ban in one of his battles (1 Sam. 15:1-35). The king was supposed to follow God (Deut. 17:18-20) but Saul did not, so God removed him Therefore God punished Saul by rejecting him and sending a troubling spirit to rob him off his peace of mind and caused temporary madness. The same case was seen in Daniel 4:28, 33 where Nebuchadnezzar was given an animal mind, his body was drenched with the dew of heaven until his hair grew like the feathers of an eagle and his nails like the claws of a bird so that he can live and eat with animals.

"Seven times will pass by for you until you acknowledge that the Most High is Sovereign over the kingdoms of men and gives them to anyone he wishes". The punishment of God could be manifested in different ways as Ananias died for lying. When God removes His protection, He often turns the person over to Satan for destruction or to an evil spirit for torment. The devil and evil spirits do this work because God has allowed them to do what come natural to them for His own. Therefore, Let no man say when he is tempted, I am tempted of God: for God cannot be tempted with evil, neither does he tempt any man: But every man is tempted, when he is drawn away of his own lust, and enticed. James 1:13-14. Even today, God is still in the business of sending evil spirit to every disobedient and obstinate heart and nation. The Evil spirit from God means punishment from God!

THE REPROBATE MIND

Reprobate is translated from the Greek word "adokimos" (pronounced ad-ok'-ee-mos), which means unapproved, rejected, and by implication worthless as Saul was rejected. The mind being our moral judge has the natural ability to distinguish between good and evil, righteousness and unrighteousness, truth and lie. It is the mind that persuades our will to determine what is good and evil but once this mind is unable to pass this moral judgment, it becomes perverse. A reprobate mind distinguishes good from evil, but influences the will to determine evil to be good. It is a degraded, depraved, immoral, evil, worthless and disapproved mind that does the things not seemly.

Examine these verses, "And even as they did not like to retain God in their knowledge, God gave them over to a reprobate mind, to do those things which are not convenient" (Romans 1:28) "Now as Jannes and Jambres withstood Moses, so do these also resist the truth: men of corrupt minds reprobate concerning the faith." (2 Timothy 3:8) "They profess that they know God; but in works they deny him, being abominable, and disobedient, and unto every good work reprobate." (Titus 1:16). The mind that perverse moral reasoning and judgment is the mind that refuses to glorify God. This mind changes the glory of the incorruptible God into an image of corruptible man and beasts.

A mind that knows the righteous judgment of God but choose to practice evil and for this, they deserve death and not only do they do these things but approve of others doing the same things. Reprobate silver shall men call them, because the LORD hath rejected them. Jeremiah 6:30. Silver that was unable to be refined was considered worthless, i.e., reprobate, and was to be rejected. Because of Israel's refusal to get right with God, they are compared to reprobate silver because God had rejected them. Rejection is only part of the definition, In Romans 1:28, we read of those who God gave over to a reprobate mind, to do those things which are not convenient. Here, the meaning is not only of rejection but abandonment.

A depraved mind is a demonic infested mind; demons will cause the fellow to bear all the possible fruits of sin, to manifest in all foolishness and corruption. It begins with idolatry, moves down to heterosexual immorality, and lastly culminates in homosexual immorality as in these days. Even the women exchanged the natural use of their bodies for that which is against nature. Men also left the natural use of the woman, burning in lust for one another, men doing with men. The sinful desires of this fellow will quicken his evil mind and letting him do things that should never be done.

His life becomes full of wickedness, as Paul says they are filled with all unrighteousness, fornication, wickedness, covetousness, maliciousness; full of envy, murder, debate, deceit, malignity; whisperers, backbiters, haters of God, despiteful, proud, boasters, inventors of evil things, disobedient to parents, without understanding, covenant breakers, without natural affection, implacable, unmerciful (Romans 1:29-31). They not only blatantly sin against God, but they have pleasure in them that do them (Romans 1:32). No, there is a great gulf fixed between the reprobate and the child of God. The reprobate becomes a backstabber, hater of God, insolent, proud, boastful and improved in inventing new ways of sinning. He is restless and deeply soaks into corruption in order that he may become fully ripe for judgment. Christians can never be reprobate if we continue in Christ's word.

Though sometimes our faith might grow weak or we possibly fall into sin, since we were purged from our old sins 2 Peter 1:9, we can never be abandoned by God. The scripture says that if we believe not, yet he abideth faithful: he cannot deny himself. (2 Timothy 2:13). In John 6:37, we read these comforting words, All that the Father giveth me shall come to me; and him that cometh to me I will in no wise cast out. The Lord Jesus has promised not cast out or reject any one who comes to him. This blessed assurance from the lips of the Savior himself leaves out any possibility of reprobation of a contrite heart. God does not commit wickedness, but He uses the wicked for His purpose for His own glory, mostly for chastisement or reproof. Let us see the wrath of God.

THE WRATH OF GOD

Still in line with seeing man as the major cause of his misfortune, failures, unrighteousness, narrow-mindedness, and retardation by giving devil a chance in his life, I wish to highlight on the wrath of God as an inevitable repercussion for every disobedience. This consciousness seems to have withered away from the mind of many, making us less than what we ought to be; Christianity without Christ and religion without truth are prerequisites for God's wrath. Mark 7:7-13. As the book of 2 Corinthians 5:11 declares, Knowing therefore the terror of the Lord, we persuade men; but we are made manifest unto God; and I trust also are made manifest in your consciences. Our God is a consuming fire, Hebrew 12:29 and His divine perfection is plainly demonstrated by what we read of in Psalm 95:11, "Unto whom I swore in my wrath."

There are two occasions of God "swearing": in making promises (Gen. 22:16) and in denouncing threatening (Deut. 1:34).

In the former, He sworn in mercy to His children; in the latter, He swore to terrify the wicked. An oath is for solemn confirmation: Hebrews 6:16. In Genesis 22:16 God said, "By Myself have I sworn." In Psalm 89:35 He declares, "Once have I sworn by my Holiness." while in Psalm 95:11 He affirmed, "I swear in my Wrath." Thus the great God Himself appeals to His "wrath" as perfection equal to His "holiness": He swore by the one as much as by the other! Again; as in Christ "dwelleth all the fullness of the Godhead bodily" (Col. 2:9), and as all the Divine perfections are illustriously displayed by Him (John 1:18), therefore His wrath is real. The mention of it terrifies many while others dismiss the thought entirely believing that a loving and merciful God could not by any means harm or destroy his creature; yes the mercy of God also speaks of His wrath. God is not ashamed to make it known that vengeance and fury belong unto Him.

He declared, "See now that I, even I am He, and there is no god with Me: I kill, and I make alive; I wound, and I heal; neither is there any that can deliver out of My hand. For I lift up My hand to heaven, and say, I live forever, If I whet my glittering sword, and mine hand take hold on judgment; I will render vengeance to mine enemies, and will reward them that hate me" (Deut. 32:39-41). That Divine wrath is one of the perfections of God is not only evident from the considerations presented above, but is also clearly established by the express declarations of His own Word. "For the wrath of God is revealed from heaven" (Rom. 1:18).

According to Robert Haldane comments on this verse: It was revealed when the sentence of death was first pronounced, the earth cursed, and man driven out of the earthly paradise; and afterwards by such examples of punishment as those of the Deluge and the destruction of the Cities of the Plain by fire from heaven; but especially by the reign of death throughout the world. It was proclaimed in the curse of the law on every transgression, and was intimated in the institution of sacrifice. In the book of Romans, the apostle calls the attention of believers to the fact that the whole creation has become subject to vanity, and groaned and travailed together in pain.

The same creation which declares that there is a God, and publishes His glory, also proclaims that He is the Enemy of sin and the Avenger of the crimes of men. But above all, the wrath of God was revealed from heaven when the Son of God came down to manifest the Divine character, and when that wrath was displayed in His sufferings and death, in a manner more awful than by all the tokens God had before given of His displeasure against sin. Besides this, the future and eternal punishment of the wicked is now declared in terms more solemn and explicit than formerly. Under the new dispensation there are two revelations given from heaven, one of wrath, the other of grace.

The truth of the Wrath of God is clearly revealed in the scriptures in the then and the now generations: whoever believes in the Son has eternal life, but whoever rejects the Son will not see life, for God's wrath remains on him ;the wrath of God is being revealed from heaven against all the godlessness and wickedness of men who suppress the truth by their wickedness and let no-one deceive you with empty words, for because of such things God's wrath comes on those who are disobedient, therefore do not be a partner with them [John 3:36,Romans 1:18,Ephesians 5:6-7].

God's wrath is one of the divine perfections because if He did not punish evil doers, He could be seen as a cohort of evil, if he compromises with the wicked, he could condone sin. In a mere human realm, the love for purity and chastity brings out the hatred for impurity and unchastity. The pity for the poor and the oppressed could bring out the anger against the oppressors of the defenseless. Thus, the wrath of God is Holiness of God in action. God hates sin because He is holy, his anger burns against sinners.

'Thou hatest all workers of iniquity and God is angry with the wicked everyday [Psalms 5:5; 7:11] in the book of Nahum 1:2-6, the Prophet pictures the wrath of God over the Assyrians: The Lord is a jealous God and avenging, the Lord is avenging and wrathful; the Lord takes vengeance on his adversaries and keeps wrath for his enemies. The Lord is slow to anger and of great might, and the Lord will by no means clear the guilty. His way is in whirlwind and storm, and the clouds are the dust of his feet.

He rebukes the sea and makes it dry, he dries up all the rivers; Bashan, Carmel wither and the bloom of Lebanon fades.

The mountains quake before him, the hills melt; the earth is laid waste before him, the world and all that dwell therein. Who can stand before his indignation? Who can endure the heat of his anger? His wrath is poured out like fire, and he breaks the rocks asunder. {Nahum 1:2-6 RSV} The very nature of God makes his wrath as real a necessity as imperatively and eternally requisite as his blessing is. The wrath of God could also be seen as the eternal judgment for all unrighteous, His displeasure and great anger against evil. Wrath of God is necessary to finally defeat Satan on this earth. By casting out Satan from heaven Michael and his angels won the first battle. The next battle in this war against Satan and his demons is to restrict the negative influence that they have on Earth. This begins first by taking out from the Earth what is good, and second by wiping out the garbage that remains. The first step is accomplished with the Rapture; the second step is accomplished during The Day of God's Wrath. Isaiah 13: 5-11 they come from a far country, from the end of heaven, even the Lord, and the weapons of his wrath to destroy all the land.

Howl for the day of Yahweh is at hand. It shall come as destruction from the almighty...Behold the day of the Lord comes, cruel both with wrath and fierce anger, to lay the land desolate: and he shall destroy the sinners thereof out of it...And I will punish the world for their evil, and the wicked for their iniquity; and I will cause the arrogance of the proud to cease, and will lay low the haughtiness of the terrible.

Isaiah 13: 12 I will make a mortal rarer than fine gold; and a man than the gold of Ophir. Isaiah 66: 15 for behold, the LORD will come in fire and His chariots like the whirlwind, to render His anger with fury, And His rebuke with flames of fire. Isaiah 66: 16 For the LORD will execute judgment by fire and by His sword on all flesh, and those slain by the LORD will be many. Zephaniah 1:18 Neither their silver nor their gold Will be able to deliver them On the day of the LORD'S wrath; And all the earth will be devoured In the fire of His jealousy, For He will make a complete end, Indeed a terrifying one, Of all the inhabitants of the earth. This is the Holiness of God stirred into action against sinners.

During the era of old Testament, the wrath of God were made manifest against evil doers; the flood was used in Noah generation, fire and brimstone from heaven against Sodom and Gomorrah, plagues and slaying of every first born against the Egyptians and in several occasions the Israelites experienced captivity and slavery in the hands of their enemies. In Numbers 21:49 the children of Israel rebelled against God and against Moses and God withdrew his protection. They happened to be passing through an area with many highly poisonous snakes, and many of the Israelites were bitten

However God's wrath is sadly, with breaking heart, giving us up to evil consequences both immediate and eternal. Apart from the eternal punishment that awaits every evil doer, the wrath of God can manifest immediately because when a man sinned he is instantly opened to harm or death resulting from the natural consequences of his choice to the attack of Satan or evil men. As sin of fornication opens you up to the venerable disease, unwanted pregnancy or even death so is the sin of murder and many other sins opens us up to a particular misfortune or the other. When we refuse God's leadership and protection, we are left to be bitten by Satan.

If a man has a stubborn and rebellious son, which will not obey the voice of his father, or the voice of his mother, and that, when they have chastened him, will not hearken unto them: Then shall his father and his mother lay hold on him, and bring him out unto the elders of his city, and unto the gate of his place; And they shall say unto the elders of his city, this our son is stubborn and rebellious, he will not obey our voice; he is a glutton and a drunkard. And all the men of his city shall stone him with stones that he dies: so shall thou put evil away from among you; and all Israel shall hear and fear says the book of (Deut. 21:18-20). God is unique in all ways, His power is omnipotent. His wisdom is a great deep. His love is unsearchable. His grace is unfathomable. His holiness is unapproachable. And like all His other perfections and attributes God's wrath is incomparable, incomprehensible, and infinite.

He created us, giving us all that we need still when we sin He chastises us for reproof and correction because of his Fatherly love. Every man that sin treads on a dangerous ground unless turns to repentance for God's patience and the gift of His Son is the greatest miracle in the world but His mercies will soon end and your feet will slide. "O that they were wise, that they understood this, that they would consider their latter end! For their rock is not as our Rock, even our enemies themselves being judges. For their vine is of the vine of Sodom and of the fields of Gomorrah: their grapes are grapes of gall, their clusters are bitter. Their wine is the poison of dragons, and the cruel venom of asps. Is not this laid up in store with me, and sealed up among my treasures?

To Me belonged vengeance and recompense; their foot shall slide in due time: for the day of their calamity is at hand, and the things that shall come upon them make haste" (Deut. 32:29, 31-35). Knowing that the wrath is real and inevitably awaiting every unrepented sinner, let us not allow God to withdraw his face from us, let us run from iniquities, let us not give devil an chance in our life and let us flee from the wrath to come" (Matt. 3:7) ere it be too late. Sin invites the wrath on us.

~ 5 ~

Demons/Fallen Angels

Do not think that deaf and dumb are only those physically disabled; for many Christians are spiritually deaf and dumb.

Demons or evil spirits are supernatural beings that have generally been described as malevolent spirit and biblically understood as angels not following God. They are frequently depicted as forces that may be conjured and insecurely controlled. There is a great deal of misunderstanding regarding the fallen angels and the demons. Many people believe these designations are simply different names for the same beings, but this is an inaccurate assumption.

There are clear differences between fallen angels and demons. Fallen angels are much more powerful than demons. We're told by Jesus to cast out demons. Yet, Jude cautions us in our confrontations with fallen angels. He says, in the very same way, these dreamers...slander celestial beings. But even the archangel Michael, when he was disputing with the devil about the body of Moses, did not dare to bring a slanderous accusation against him, but said, "The Lord rebuke you" (Jude 8-9) Demons are the powers of this dark world while fallen angels are the spiritual forces of evil in heavenly realms, according to Ephesians 6:12 For our struggle is not against flesh and blood, but against the rulers, against the authorities, against the powers of this dark world and against the spiritual forces of evil in the heavenly realms.

Fallen angels have their own celestial bodies; therefore they have no need to inhabit bodies. Yet demons seek bodies desperately; and, if need be, they will settle for the bodies of animals. In Mark 5:9-13: Jesus asked him, what is your name? My name is Legion, he replied, for we are many. And he begged Jesus again and again not to send them out of the area but a large herd of pigs was feeding on the nearby hillside. The demons begged Jesus, Send us among the pigs; allow us to go into them. He gave them permission, and the evil spirits came out and went into the pigs.

The herd, about two thousand in number, rushed down the steep bank into the lake and was drowned. The urgency that the spirits expressed not to be sent away, but rather to be sent into the pigs, suggests that any body (even a pig) was better than being disembodied. Ironically, their sudden entrance into the pigs caused the pigs to panic, rush into the sea, and drown. In Matt 12:43-45: when an evil spirit comes out of a man, it goes through arid places seeking rest and does not find it. Then it says, I will return to the house I left. When it arrives, it finds the house unoccupied, swept clean and put in order.

Then it goes and takes with it seven other spirits more wicked than itself, and they go in and live there. And the final condition of that man is worse than the first. Here Jesus taught of demons, or evil spirits, as beings who cannot find rest in dry places, but urgently seeks to return to the body it has left. If the person from whom the spirit was expelled does not take certain measures, the demon will return and bring seven others more evil than himself into his house.

These scriptures just cited strongly suggest that demons are disembodied spirits, not angels. In Ephesians 6:12 we can clearly see a described satanic hierarchy, a chain of command. In descending order of rank we find Rulers (Principalities), Authorities, Powers of this Dark World, and (last of all), spiritual forces of evil in the heavenly (or invisible spiritual) realms. Fallen angels have the ability to fly, but demons can only walk. Jesus says concerning demons, "When the unclean spirit is gone out of a man, he walketh through dry places, seeking rest, and findeth none" (Matthew 12:43).

In this context, we shall scripturally examine the origin of these evil entities. The Scriptures did not explicitly tell us when the angelic realm was created but the only available information implies that the angels were formed after God created the heavens but before he fashioned the earth. Passages from Job and Nehemiah seem to bolster this view: Job 38:4 "Where were you when I laid the foundation of the earth? Tell me, if you have understanding, 5 who set its measurements? Since you know, or who stretched the line on it? 6 On what were its bases sunk? Or who laid its cornerstone, 7 when the morning stars sang together and all the sons of God shouted for joy? Nehemiah 9:6 You alone are the Lord; You have made heaven, the heaven of heavens, with all their host, the earth and everything on it, the seas and all that is in them, and You preserve them all. The host of heaven worships You.

The expressions "morning stars" and "sons of God" used in Job 38:7 refer to the angels, So does the phrase "host of heaven" used in Nehemiah 9:6. These passages indicate that the angelic domain was created after the heavens, but before the earth was given final form. Very soon after the creation, Satan a powerful and high-ranking angel sinned. His fall from grace is the first instance documented in the Bible of angels disobeying God at which he and other angels were sent out of Heaven, but it is not the only one. There is another incident recorded in Genesis 6 which occurred soon after Satan's rebellion:

Genesis 6:1 when men began to increase in number on the earth and daughters were born to them, 2 the sons of God saw that the daughters of men were beautiful, and they married any of them they chose. 4 The Nephilim were on the earth in those days and also afterward when the sons of God went to the daughters of men and had children by them. They were the heroes of old, men of renown. Just as it did in Job 38:7, the term "sons of God" in Genesis 6:2, 4 refer to the angels.

Satan once was called the morning star (Lucifer), which identifies him with the angels. He was among the morning stars that sang for joy when God created the universe. All the angels are also called the sons of God. After the angels sinned by marrying human women, they bore them gigantic hybrid children. The Bible calls these offspring; nephilim, the "mighty men of old, warriors of renown" (Gen. 6:4). When they appear again later in the Scriptures, they are called by a variety of names, including Rephaim, Zumim, Emim and Horites (Gen. 14:5), Anakim (Deut. 2:11), Zamzummim (Deut. 2:20), and Avim (Deut. 2:23). The name Nephilim does not only mean giants, but it also carries with it the meaning of tormentors, bullies, and tyrants. So just the name itself implies that these are demon spirits.

However God expressed His wrath on these angels that sinned as recorded in the book of Jude 6 "And the angels who did not keep their own position, but left their proper dwelling, he has kept in eternal chains in deepest darkness for the judgment of the great Day, II Peter 2:4 for indeed God did not spare the angels who sinned, but cast them down in chains of darkness into the low regions and delivered them to be kept for the judgment of torment And I Peter 3:19 . . . He went and preached to the spirits in prison, 20 who formerly were disobedient, when once the Divine longsuffering waited in the days of Noah, while the ark was being prepared, in which a few, that is, eight souls, were saved through water.

Since the hybrid nephilim (offspring of angels and daughters of men) had both physical and spiritual natures, they were able to survive the deaths of their physical bodies. These hybrid spirits had nowhere to go when their physical existence ceased, thus they began to seek for bodies to occupy. Demons are these disembodied spirits of the Nephilim who were destroyed in the flood, yet their spirits remained on the earth as in Genesis chapter six. The Nephilim are the offspring of fallen angels and humans. This is the clear difference between fallen angels and demons. Fallen angles do not seek to inhabit the body but demons desperately seek a body to occupy be it human or animal because their bodies were destroyed during the flood. Someone might object by saying, "But Jesus said that angels do not have sex, so how could the term sons of God be referring to angels?"

Let's look at the passage carefully where Jesus discussed this: Jesus replied, "The people of this age marry and are given in marriage. But those who are considered worthy of taking part in that age and in the resurrection from the dead will neither marry nor be given in marriage, and they can never die; for they are like the angels. They are God's children, since they are children of the resurrection Luke 20:34-37. The way Luke puts the words of Christ, humans will be like the angels because they can never die, not because they can never marry. However, the way Matthew constructs the sentence, it appears different: At the resurrection people will neither marry nor be given in marriage; they will be like the angels in heaven. (Matthew 22:30) "You see," someone may argue, "angels can't marry, so the sons of God could not refer to angels because the sons of God married."

Before someone debates this point, they should take note that only the angels in heaven don't marry. There is no mentioned about the angels who were cast out of heaven. Finally, it is the departed spirits of the nephilim that became what we know as "demons." These entities are mentioned in the Old Testament (for example, see Lev. 17:7; Deut. 32:17; II Chr. 11:15; Psa. 106:37), and numerous times in the New Testament, where they are called "demons," "unclean spirits," and "evil spirits." The scripture has many names to describe these demons:

DEAF AND DUMB SPIRIT

This spirit that operates with that stronghold centered on making Christians spiritually deaf and dumb to the voice and revelation of God. The way that this spirit accomplishes its work is by becoming a stronghold of the mind, better known as a mindset. It will make you dumb so that you cannot understand the truth of God's word, or voice of the Holy Spirit. It is also connected to learning disabilities, attention deficit disorder, dyslexia, memory conditions, concentration, spiritual deafness, and physical deafness.

The dumb spirit affects your ability to understand revelation. It makes you spiritually dumb, that you cannot understand the revelation of the spirit of wisdom and revelation. It affects your ability to understand the Bible and Spiritual mysteries. When you are deaf and dumb in the spirit, you have nothing good to say. So there is a form of godliness, denying the power. When we are spiritually deaf and dumb, we do what we do now because we have done it for the last ten years. We talk about power, but we do not see the manifestation. We talk about what we did 20 years ago, but we do not see anything.

We talk about the truth of the gospel and proclaim that Jesus is the same yesterday, today and forever, but we do not see anything. We are hearers, and not doers. The bible declares, let him who has an ear hear what the Spirit is saying. We can only what the Spirit is saying when our spiritual ears are open. Do you think the devil wants you to hear the voice of God? Do you think the devil is going to have demons such as epilepsy, infirmity, sickness, pain and torment and every other devil in hell and not have a counter-attack? No!

This spirit wars against the message and faith. Without faith it is impossible to please God. Whatever you ask for, praying and believing, you will receive it. The devil does not want you to have faith. He knows the power of faith. He knows the kingdom of God operates by the law and principal of faith. Romans 10:17 recorded; so faith comes from hearing, and hearing by the word of Christ. He wants to get your hearing. You will read the word, but you do not hear. No matter how many times you read, you will be a hearer only and not a doer. You want to be a doer but you do not know why you are not a doer. You do not know why you do not believe what you proclaim.

You confess it, but right inside you do not believe it anymore because nothing has happen. What is the problem? There is a spirit that has blocked your spiritual ears, every word from the preacher sounds like a mere fiction or fairytale. Every time the message of the kingdom comes, this spirit comes to rob you of those seeds of revelation, which can give you faith. We must get the revelation out of our head and into our heart, but we cannot because of the spiritual assignment; the principality called the deaf spirit. Our faith comes only by hearing! How many times have your Pastor preached about sin and holiness? Do not think that deaf and dumb are only those physically disabled for many Christians are spiritually deaf and dumb.

And they brought the boy to Him. And when he saw Him, immediately the spirit threw him into a convulsion, and falling to the ground, he began rolling about and foaming at the mouth. And He asked his father, How long has this been happening to him? And he said, from childhood. And it has often thrown him both into the fire and into the water to destroy him. But if you can do anything... Mark 9:20-22

See the hopelessness and disappointment? The man did not have much faith, confidence or hope. That spirit of this man was speaking through his heart when he said, if you can do anything. Look at the first thing that Jesus said. It looks a little brutal. Mark 9:23 And Jesus said to him, if you can! All things are possible to him who believes. Not if I can do anything, but if you believe. All things are possible to them who believe. Then, we see the mercy of God. Mark 9:24. Immediately the boy's father cried out and began saying, I do believe, help my unbelief. That means that the father's unbelief helped keep his boy bound to sickness. We see that the deaf and dumb spirit is connected to unbelief. It is connected to the hindrances of our healing. Mark 9:25 recorded that when Jesus saw that a crowd was rapidly gathering, He rebuked the unclean spirit, saying to it, You deaf and dumb spirit, I command you, come out of him and do not enter him again.

When Jesus calls the demon a deaf and dumb spirit. I thought it was an epileptic or mute spirit. After unbelief is revealed, He reveals that the power of the spirit of unbelief is broken because unbelief is repented of and faith is revealed. The spirit of unbelief is what gives strength to a spirit that makes men deaf, dumb and mute. After the unbelief is dealt with, Jesus is able to get to the root; the deaf and dumb spirit. We need not only repent of personal unbelief but also like Daniel, confess the sins of a nation (generational unbelief) and walk in the contrary, the spirit of Faith. Read the book of Mark 9 vs.17-29.

PERVERSE SPIRIT

The word perversion means to make crooked, to do amiss, to bow down, to commit iniquity, to pervert, to trouble and to do wrong. The strong-man of perversion is characterized primarily by hate towards God; inability to do God's will and having a broken spirit. The ultimate form of perversion is an atheist, who has perverted everything God intended for his life: instead of serving and worshipping the Lord, he does just the opposite. The spirit of perversion is the spirit of error. The Bible says, "the Lord hath mingled a perverse spirit in the midst thereof: and they have caused Egypt to err in every work thereof, as drunken man staggered in his vomit "Isaiah 19:14. Very often, this brings about doctrinal error in the mist of believers. When we do things on our own way rather than following God's will, we are perverting or twisting the word of God.   In the same way the men also abandoned natural relations with women and were inflamed with **lust** for one another. Men commit indecent acts with other men, and receive in themselves the due penalty for their perversion.

If you or someone you know is dealing with a perverse spirit, speak to God in the name of Jesus to help you or that person change their ways. God loves you and that person more than you can ever understand and He has demonstrated it by creating us to have power to speak to and change our situations. There are angels ready to fight the battle for you. I pray right now that anyone dealing with a perverse spirit be set free in the name of Jesus and by faith I know that the Holy Spirit will help them gain a new understanding of a better way of life. Isaiah 19:14; Romans 1:17-32

SPIRIT OF ERROR

Just as Apostle John earlier said; Beloved, do not believe every spirit, but test the spirits, whether they are of God; because many false prophets have gone out into the world. By this you know the Spirit of God: every spirit that confesses that Jesus Christ has come in the flesh is of God, and every spirit that does not confess that Jesus Christ has come in the flesh is not of God. And this is the spirit of the Antichrist, which you have heard was coming, and is now already in the world. You are of God, little children, and have overcome them, because He who is in you is greater than he who is in the world. They are of the world. Therefore they speak as of the world, and the world hears them. We are of God. He who knows God hears us; he who is not of God does not hear us. By this we know the spirit of truth and the spirit of error.1 John 4:6.

Throughout the first epistle of John, it is clear that the apostle is concerned about Christians being deceived. He wrote with urgency to warn them about anti-Christ in chapter two. In that context the writer said, "no lie is of the truth," and he said, "Who is a liar but he who denies that Jesus is the Christ?" In chapter three, verse seven he said: "Let no one deceive you." John was not an alarmist or paranoid. But he entertained a realistic concern about Christians being deceived; he knew the spirit of error as opposed to the spirit of truth. If that reality escapes our notice, we are in trouble today. "Beloved, do not believe every spirit, but test the spirits, whether they are of God; because many false prophets have gone out into the world." We cannot just accept anyone who claims they have the Spirit; we cannot just let our minds fall under the influence of any spirit. It may be the spirit of error. The only way to know is to read the Word of God. You cannot believe everything you hear! Be from politics, medicine, science, history or computer.

What about religion? Can you believe everything you hear? If you listen to the various religious messages about in the world today, you soon discover messages in conflict. All you hear cannot be the truth. All you hear cannot be taught in the Scriptures by God. Some theological systems maintain that we are predestined, without regard to the personal will of heart. Others have built a sacramental system, surrounded by traditions and man-made doctrine and practice. At large in "evangelical" religion, there is a primary concentration on belief in Christ, but often denying the role of baptism and downplaying obedience to the teachings of the apostles. Religious cults claim authority in their writings and structure. Human creeds are enforced. Some in world religions deny that Jesus Christ is the Savior, the Only Begotten Son of God. Do we just believe everything we hear? The messages in modern religion are in conflict. John says: Do not believe everybody who claims they are telling you what you ought to believe and do in religion! Do not accept every teacher's claim that he is telling you what the Holy Spirit revealed. Try the spirits; test all religious teaching!

Let me ask you ~ which religious teachers today, should we apply this test to?? Every single one of them! Billy Graham, Benny Hinn, Jerry Falwell, Max Lucado, Charles Swindoll, Warren Berkley and every other preacher or teacher you might listen to, and every uninspired author you read. Every single religious teacher should be tested in the same way, by simply seeing if what he says is in the Scriptures! Let me state the matter in these terms: Never think that if a man is popular and brings in huge crowds that mean he must be teaching the truth! Never think that if a man is a good public speaker and can hold the attention of an audience that means he must be teaching the truth.

Never think that if you like the person, he must be teaching the truth. Never think that if a man has been baptized and is a member of a local church of Christ, he has to be a perfect teacher of truth. Never thinks that if a man quotes a lot of Scripture, he must be teaching the truth. Never think that if a man has academic, educational credentials, he must be teaching the truth!! It is a mistake to decide you like the man; therefore you'll accept everything he says. The better approach is take the message, compare that message with what is revealed; then accept the message not because of the man, but because it is revealed. There is only one way to determine if a man is teaching the truth - - see if what he says is in the Bible!! In order for you to make that determination you know what you'll have to do? Read and study your Bible!

SPIRIT OF HEAVINESS

A spirit of heaviness causes depression, feeling dopey, sleepy, or feeling drugged. A spirit of heaviness causes spiritually the inability to pray or read the Bible. A spirit of heaviness vomits into your ear gossip, slander, criticism, judgment, and condemnation. A spirit of heaviness causes you to sleep in church, when you try to pray or read the word of God. It darkens your countenance and makes hearts are downcast. It brings a heavy, oppressive feeling just to quench your faith. Sometimes, it may come over many at once, like a cloud, hanging over a place.

It causes you to isolate, steals your love, and make you feel alone. It is a similar sort of feeling that businessmen get today when they see business dwindling and difficulties multiplying. Indeed all mankind to some extent are afflicted with the spirit of heaviness when they contemplate world conditions with any seriousness. Jesus explained this, saying that men's hearts would fail them for fear as they look ahead to the things which are coming upon the earth. (Luke 21:26) It is that depressed attitude of mind which results from fear of the unknown future. The counterattack against the enemy is to command it to loose your body, don't believe anything negative about yourself. Accept no criticism of yourself or others. The book of 2 Corinthians 10:5 instructs us to destroy arguments and every proud obstacle to the knowledge of God, and take every thought captive to obey Christ, finally, put on the garment of praise as declared in Isaiah 61:3. Put on praise music and praise, praise, praise until the heaviness lifts off of you.

SPIRIT OF JEALOUSY

Jealousy typically refers to the negative or angry thoughts, feelings, and behaviors of insecurity, fear, and anxiety that occur when a person believes a valued relationship is being threatened by a rival, or when another person is perceived to have some type of advantage. Jealousy often contains a mixture of emotions such as anger, sadness, disgust, which are focused by passion or anger.

While jealousy and envy are similar, they differ in that jealousy concerns something one has and is afraid of losing, while envy concerns something one does not have and either he wants to acquire, or prevent another person from getting it. Jealousy is about real or imagined fears--fear of abandonment, fear of loss of love, fear of being dishonored in the relationship, fear of being shamed in the community, unresolved issues from past relationships, lack issues, poor self esteem, cover or mask for things from the past that you haven't healed yet, vindictive or a desire for revenge that is misguided or misdirected toward someone else.

When jealous feelings come up, it's usually because we're afraid that we won't get our needs of one kind or another met. It's been our experience that when jealousy comes up, somewhere within us we are crying out for help. These are the negative connotation of the word jealousy; however, in the Bible we find that there is such thing as righteous jealousy. So before we get into the effects of sinful jealousy and how to have victory over it, we'll examine some different types of jealousy. God is jealous. He has a right--there is no God but Him. Christians are wedded to Him and we should not go a whoring after other gods. A betrothal is a marriage and all who claim to be Christians claim to be the Bride of Christ. Marriage is a binding contract. God is only as good as His Word, and he takes us at our Word.

A woman serves God as she obeys her husband (Genesis 3:16; I Peter 3:6). If we claim to be the wife of Christ He expects us to obey His Word, and every one. As a husband is head of his wife and takes her responsibility upon his shoulder, so Christ is head of the Church, and we obey Him, the Word, in everything.

Exodus 34:14, for thou shall worship no other god: for the LORD, whose name is Jealous, is a jealous God. A man with a suspected unfaithful spouse is jealous. He has a right to know if his beloved is being faithful or adulterous. When a man proposes marriage to a woman and she says 'yes', they are married at that point in time. As Christians they will not consummate the marriage until they have asked the Lord's blessing, celebrated by the witness of family and friends, and met the requirements of the state. But the moment she accepts his proposal, the two are married. If she should change her mind and marry another, she shall be called an adulteress.

No woman can have more than one living husband (Romans7vs.1-3) Numbers 5:12; Speak unto the children of Israel, and say unto them, If any man's wife go aside, and commit a trespass against him, 5:13 And a man lie with her carnally, and it be hid from the eyes of her husband, and be kept close, and she be defiled, and there be no witness against her, neither she be taken with the manner; 5:14 And the spirit of jealousy come upon him, and he be jealous of his wife, and she be defiled: or if the spirit of jealousy come upon him, and he be jealous of his wife, and she be not defiled: (procedure to determine her guilt/innocence found in verses 15-31)

3. A man jealous for the Lord. This person gives his exclusive loyalty to God. 1 Kings 19:10, And he [Elijah] said, I have been

very jealous for the LORD God of hosts: for the children of Israel have forsaken thy covenant, thrown down thine altars, and slain thy prophets with the sword; and I, even I only, am left; and they seek my life, to take it away.

4. A man with godly jealousy. This person has led someone to Christ and wants them to stay on track with Jesus. It could also be a Christian worker who wants to see those he helps stay with Jesus. 2 Corinthians 11:2, For I [Paul] am jealous over you with godly jealousy: for I have espoused you to one husband that I may present you as a chaste virgin to Christ. Sinful jealousy is resentfully envious. Song of Solomon 8:6 ...jealousy is cruel as the grave. Jealousy provokes us to anger and it is the rage of a man... No good can come from such anger, because the wrath of man worked not the righteousness of God.

Let us see the accounts of Moses and Korah:

Num 16:1 Now Korah, the son of Izhar, the son of Kohath, the son of Levi, and Dathan and Abiram, the sons of Eliab, and On the son of Peleth, sons of Reuben, took men: 2 And they rose up before Moses, with certain of the children of Israel, two hundred and fifty princes of the assembly, famous in the congregation, men of renown: 3 And they gathered themselves together against Moses and against Aaron, and said unto them, Ye take too much upon you, seeing all the congregation are holy, every one of them, and the LORD is among them: wherefore then lift ye up yourselves above the congregation of the LORD?

Please note that Korah was a man of fame and renown in the congregation. This spirit walks with those with Jezebel (spirit of control and rebellion/witchcraft) and who love to be recognized in the congregation (yes they are born again children of the Lord). This spirit comes against those called out of the Lord to true leadership, as was Moses. They do not come against those who have promoted themselves to leadership in the congregation, but against those with the anointing of spiritual leadership by the calling of the Most High God. Those that walk with a heart of love and servant-hood, those who are aware that they themselves are nothing and are capable of no good thing, save for Christ Jesus living in them and flowing through them.

I perceive that we will see more and more of this spirit manifest as the truly anointed Prophets and Apostles are released from their hidden places. It is a spirit of spiritual jealousy. It says we are all children of God and who do you think you are? Why should you have the anointing of leadership? Who are you to tell us what to do and what is error? Why should you have anointing that we don't have? It will attempt to dominate the conversation so as to show how spiritual they are and will cut one off and bring the subject back to them selves quickly (this is also a manifestation of the spirit of pride, both in the world and in the church). It will cut off with a glare or an abrupt change in conversation if the one called to leadership dare share what the Lord is doing in and through them, or dare share a revelation.

This spirit causes their spiritual hearts and minds to literally close down so that the truth cannot reach them i.e. the things that are shared are met with a blank stare and the question is raised of what do you know? I know it all! It walks with the spirit of pride, Leviathan and the spirit of control, Jezebel. It will use words that sound spiritually correct i.e. you lift yourself up and are full of spiritual pride, so as to cut that one called to leadership down. Their words will cut you to the bone and spiritually deeply drain you. Korah did that to Moses and Moses fell on his face! Num 16:4 and when Moses heard it, he fell upon his face.

Once this sin overcomes us, we begin robbing God of His time; we automatically stay focused on the response of others instead of good fruits we ought to be bear. Jealousy interrupts our fellowship with God. Jesus commands that we make peace with those we are angry with before coming to God with a gift. If you are jealous and angry you are not coming to God with a clean heart. The book of Matthew 5:22-24 declared that whosoever is angry with his brother without a cause shall be in danger of the judgment... Therefore if thou bring thy gift to the altar, and there remembers that thy brother hath ought against thee; Leave there thy gift before the altar, and go thy way; first be reconciled to thy brother, and then come and offer thy gift. Jealousy can cause hatred. That is like committing murder. Same was with I John 3:15, whosoever hateth his brother is a murderer.

We cannot love God and hate our brother. I John 4:20 if a man say, I love God, and hateth his brother, he is a liar: for he that loveth not his brother whom he hath seen, how can he love God whom he hath not seen? Jealousy is oftentimes tied to the sins of envy (feeling of discontent because of another's advantage) and/or covetousness (to ardently desire something that someone else has). When we nurse jealousy, and don't rebuke it, we willingly sin. James 4:17 Therefore to him that knoweth to do good, and doeth it not, to him it is sin.

Jealousy is consuming and can become an idol. The mind thinks on it, sometimes we may try to "outdo" the object of our jealousy, and our relationship with God suffers. Our fixation should be on Jesus, not another human being.

Overcoming Spirit of Jealousy

Christians are already over-comers because of what Christ did when He made an open show of the dark powers and principalities of this world. You no longer have to be subject to your flesh, the devil, or the world. Thanks be to God, who gives us the victory through our Lord Jesus Christ.

To overcome the spirit of jealousy, you must:

1. Submit yourself to God by stepping up your Bible studies. Try Proverbs which has a lot of practical everyday wisdom on how we should behave wisely. Remember God is speaking to you through His word. Follow what it says.

2. Fast for the problem and look for God's answer. It's coming.

3. Pray fervently for humility, meekness, contrite heart, and charity.

4. Take it one day at a time (Matthew 6:34) and one transaction at a time.

When a circumstance comes up where you might get jealous, begin to pray to God silently.

You can say, "God loves this person, Jesus loves this person, I love this person." You can even quote scripture.

5. During prayer, tell God, out loud, that you love the person you are jealous of and to make it so in your heart. He commanded us to love. Love is not emotion; it is an act of the will. We make the decision to love. As time goes on, this decision becomes heartfelt love through God.

6. Through reading the Bible, understand who you are in Christ and how all things are yours. Our sense of worth is defined by what we are in Christ, not by what we are in this world or the eyes of other people.

7. Take all of your deepest feelings to the Lord in prayer. Humble yourself by getting down on your knees. Talk to the Lord out loud. Don't be embarrassed--He already knows your feelings and wants you to share with Him. Cast all your care upon Him for he careth for you (I Peter 5:7).

8. Determine, like Paul, that you will not be brought under the power of anything (I Corinthians 6:12) and that you will keep your body under subjection (1 Corinthians 9:27)

9. If you do not currently have a ministry for the Lord, get one and work. Serving other people minimizes your own problems and gives you honor by being a fellow laborer with the Lord.

10. Meditate on the word of God continually. This has a cleansing effect.

11. Disassociate yourself with ungodly things or people that feed your jealousy.

SPIRIT OF INFIRMITY

When we read that expression, "spirit of infirmity," many of us just pass over it. Understanding the relationship between demon activities and sickness in the bodies of the children of God will clearly highlight the meaning of 'spirit of infirmity. The spirit of infirmity manifests mainly as a deaf and dumb spirit in regards to learning disabilities, bi-polar disorder, schizophrenia, memory loss, the inability to focus, other memory problems. The book of Luke 13:12 recorded a woman that had an infirmity. Jesus said to her, "Woman, you are loosed from your infirmity."Being bent over in stature means an infirmity is in the spine. If that woman had lived today and had gone to the best clinic in the land to get a diagnosis, they would have diagnosed her with arthritis in her backbone, curvature of the spinal column, slipped disc, etc..

But nobody would have diagnosed that woman with having an evil spirit. Luke, who recorded this event, recognized that Satan is the author of sickness. Infirmity can appear as weakness, robbed, grieved, wounded, defective, physical weakness, weak in old age or disease or feeble or lacking a firmness of will, character, or purpose. Hope deferred in the mind causes weakness and frailty; the heart becomes sick, then depression sets in. The medical profession calls it fibromyalgia. The person can't think straight also may suffer from extreme pain over different parts of their body.

Numerous Scriptures verified the assertion that some sicknesses are demonic. *Matt 8:1616 When the even was come, they brought unto him many that were possessed with devils: and he cast out the spirits with his word, and healed all that were sick: Matt 9:32-3332 As they went out, behold, they brought to him a dumb man possessed with a devil. 33 And when the devil was cast out, the dumb spake: and the multitudes marveled, saying, It was never so seen in Israel.*

Matt 12:2222 Then was brought unto him one possessed with a devil, blind, and dumb: and he healed him, insomuch that the blind and dumb both spake and saw. Mark 1:23-2523 And there was in their synagogue a man with an unclean spirit; and he cried out, 24 Saying, Let us alone; what have we to do with thee, thou Jesus of Nazareth? art thou come to destroy us? I know thee who thou art, the Holy One of God. 25 And Jesus rebuked him, saying, Hold thy peace, and come out of him. Mark 9:2525 When Jesus saw that the people came running together, he rebuked the foul spirit, saying unto him, Thou dumb and deaf spirit, I charge thee, come out of him, and enter no more into him.

Luke 4:3535 and Jesus rebuked him, saying, Hold thy peace, and come out of him. And when the devil had thrown him in the midst, he came out of him, and hurt him not. Luke 9:11 Then he called his twelve disciples together, and gave them power and authority over all devils, and to cure diseases. Luke 10:1919 Behold, I give unto you power to tread on serpents and scorpions, and over all the power of the enemy: and nothing shall by any means hurt you. Luke 13:1111 And, behold, there was a woman which had a spirit of infirmity eighteen years, and was bowed together, and could in no wise lift up herself. Acts 10:38 How God anointed Jesus of Nazareth with the Holy Ghost and with power: who went about doing good, and healing all that were oppressed of the devil; for God was with him. Eph 6:12 For we wrestle not against flesh and blood, but against principalities, against powers, against the rulers of the darkness of this world, against spiritual wickedness in high places. For more detail, see Demons and Sickness.

SPIRIT OF HAUGHTINESS

Haughtiness, pride, arrogance, ego, self-exaltation or self-will is simply placing yourself as God, acting like it's all up to you and your power. This is the same spirit that made Satan rebelled against God. God opposes the proud but gives grace to the humble." Haughty people seek their own glory not the glory of God.

They never ask for help; never need a handout; never vulnerable, always strong, don't want to ask for directions, never show tears. Haughtiness never admits a mistake and cannot apologize.

It always wants to be recognized, applauded, admired and celebrated. Haughtiness wants people to "See how wonderful I am". You want people to know your titles and degrees, your popularity, your talents; to know how busy you are, how important you are ,you want people to admire how wise and spiritual, vulnerable and mature you are; just like Pharisees, wanting seats of honor and recognition. Luke 18:11-12, the Pharisee stood up and prayed about himself: 'God, I thank you that I am not like other men— robbers, evildoers, adulterers—or even like this tax collector. I fast twice a week and give a tenth of all I get.

Haughtiness is superiority complex. The "I am better, wealthier, smarter, more successful and more righteous than you, spirit. Simply because you'll be travelling to USA tomorrow, next week Japan and next month Australia, you loudly sang it out that everyone in your Church may know you are connected. The Bible calls this pride.

Now listen, you who say, "Today or tomorrow we will go to this or that city, spend a year there, carry on business and make money." Why, you do not even know what will happen tomorrow. What is your life? You are a mist that appears for a little while and then vanishes. 15 Instead, you ought to say, "If it is the Lord's will, we will live and do this or that." As it is, you boast and brag. All such boasting is evil (James 4:13-16).

We Must Recognize Our Sinfulness not like the Pharisee trusted in himself that he was righteous, prayed with himself, thanking God he was better than other people, but like the Publican pleaded for mercy admitting he was a sinner. Note the conclusion in v14 - One who exalts self will be abased; one who humbles self will be exalted! Humility is the opposite of self-exaltation and self-righteousness.

We must depend on God just like Moses knew that man lives, not by bread alone, but by the word of God. Our physical blessings come, not by our own power and might, but from God. All good things come from God. We must appreciate how weak we would be without Him. This leads us to depend on God to meet our needs. In turn, we then appreciate and exalt Him. Deuteronomy 8:3, 11-14, 16-18 We Must Submit To God's Commands. If we know our weaknesses and our tendency to err, in contrast to God's wisdom and power, we should be willing to do what He says. We should believe that His will is best and that we will receive His aid only if we obey Him. As Christians we must accept circumstances of life according to God's will. A meek and humble person will accept persecution, mistreatment, suffering, or hardship without rebelling against God and without doubting His wisdom.

We will accept the fact that He has chosen to allow this to happen for His good purposes. Numbers 11:10-15 - Moses had problems most of us would never submit to. People constantly complained about his leadership, even though he was just doing what God said. How many of us would have stood for it? No wonder he was called the meekest man on earth!   In fact, it was a complaint against him that occasioned the statement that he was so meek (12:1-3). Christ Jesus led example of Humility for us. He was led as a sheep to the slaughter Acts 8:32, 33, Isaiah 53:7. Matthew 26:39 - Was it hard for Jesus to go to the "slaughter"? Did this take meekness? He said, "Not my will but thine be done. In Philippians 2:8 it was recorded that Jesus left the glory of heaven, humbled Himself and became obedient to the point of the death on the cross. Consider how much humility and meekness would be required for one to willingly leave the glory of heaven to come to earth to live as a man and die as a criminal to save others. Others names of demons which will not be treated in this text include:

Spirit of whoredom: Hosea 4:12-26, **Evil spirit:** Luke 7 vs.21; Acts 19 vs.12-13

Familiar spirit: 1 Samuel 28 vs.7, **Foul spirit:** Mark 9:25, **Seducing spirit** 1Timothy 4:1

Spirit of an unclean devil: Luke 4:33, **Spirit of antichrist:** 1 Corinthians 10:10; 15:26

Spirit of fear: 11 Timothy 1:7, **Spirit of Slumber:** Isaiah 29:10; Romans 11:8

Unclean Spirit: Mark 6:7; Luke 11:24-26, **Giants** Genesis 6:4

Sons of the Most High: Psalms 82:6 **Satyres:** Isaiah 13:21, 34:14, **Serpents and Scorpions** Luke 10:19, **Dominion, Principalities, Powers, Rulers of this world Spiritual Wickedness in High Places.** Ephesians 6:12, Colossians 1:16, Colossians 2:15 and Ephesians 1:21.

Demons can cause mental illness; give the body superhuman strength, stimulating physical disabilities and sickness like blindness, deafness etc. They can speak through the vocal chords of the person they possess, often strange languages; causing the person to become mentally unstable or even suicidal. Demons possess personalities and intelligence. Matthew 8:31. Luke 4:35, 41. James 2:19.

They are Satan's messengers and communication devices. Matthew 12:22-30. Demons are multitude in number...Mark 5:5. They are beings of a very low moral, debased in character and moral principle. They represent some degrees of moral wickedness as returning to their former abode takes with themselves seven other spirits that are more wicked. Matthew 12:42-43. They are foul spirits, unclean, sullen, violent and malicious. Luke 6:18. 8:39, Matt 10:1. 12:43. Mk 1:23, 24. Whether demons are fallen angels, or lesser spirits of a different origin, they will evidently share the final destiny of their master, Satan.

Jesus said that the everlasting fire, into which they will be thrown, was prepared for the Devil and his angels: Then he will say to those on his left, Depart from me, you who are cursed, into the eternal fire prepared for the devil and his angels (Matt. 25:41). Even if demons are not the same as angels, they may still be included in their number. The word for angel in Greek, means messenger, and may include all of Satan's quote messengers (II Cor. 12:7). Presently demons and evil angels are free to operate on the earth but time shall come when they will be bound, so that they can no longer deceive the nations.

One class of rebellious angels, possibly those mentioned in Genesis chapter 6, are not free, but are kept bound unto judgment in a place called Tartaros in Greek. II Pet. 2:4: ...God did not spare angels when they sinned, but sent them to hell [Gk. Tartaros], putting them into gloomy dungeons to be held for judgment... (See also Jude 6) **Every demon bows at the mention of the name of lord Jesus Christ**- Philippians 2: 10.

ATTRIBUTES OF DEMONS

Inducement into evil:

"More subtle than any other wild creature." The craftiness of Satan and his cohorts is evident right from the beginning of creation. They always try to access our mind and to entice us with our immediate desire. As each person is tempted when he is lured and enticed by his own desire. Then desire when it has conceived gives birth to sin; and sin when it is full-grown brings forth death. {James 1:14-15} Satan will never appear with horns, hoof, and a tail, announcing his arrival, rather parades himself like an angel of light, making evil appear good. We are often enticed to sin through the following :{ I John. 2:16}

- [a]lust of the eyes -self aspiration
- [b]lust of the flesh -self gratification
- [c]boastful pride of life- self reputation: I Timothy 4:1, 2 Timothy 3:13, Proverbs 1:10

Enslavement of the mind and body:

This could be seen as possession. It is the outright control of human personality by the power of a wicked spirit. It also extends to such activities as soothsaying, occultism, spiritism (or spiritualism), and related black magic arts such as astrology, fortune telling and the like. The evil spirits tries acquiring power over the nerves and will of man, like a great wall between the body and soul bridging the sense of communication so that a person loses control over his conscious and unconscious actions. When the control of the body is lost, the evil spirit enthralls the man making him a slave to all his desires. However, the soul can think or feel but has no power and control over the body. In this state, it is very difficult to remember dreams or visions. In some cases, the possessed causes harm to himself or pose danger to the environment as in Matthew. 17:15; Mark 5:4 and Luke 13:11

Deception into falsehood:

Evil spirit has deceived many and they are still in the business of deceit. The possessed exhibit prophesies and the supposed ability to perceive things that are usually beyond the range of human senses. The book of Acts recorded a young woman who earned good money for her masters by telling people their future but when she was delivered by Paul, she lost her clairvoyant abilities (Acts 16:16-19).

~ 6 ~

DEMONS AND ADDICTIONS

*They promise them freedom, while they
themselves are slaves of depravity, for a man
is a slave to whatever has mastered him.*

Addiction is a persistent and compulsive dependence on a behavior or substance despite harm. This term has been partially replaced by the word dependence for substance abuse. Although it has been extended to include mood-altering behaviors or activities that force some degree of servitude and sacrifice to the addicting victim; it is also imperative to know that addiction is highly vulnerable to spiritual influences. To distinguish these facts, when one is possessed, his will and mind beings are controlled by demonic influences; he loses control of his action and is wholly turned a slave to his desire. The only outstanding difference between addiction and possession is that the former might depend on a substance while the latter is wholly a stronghold of the mind and will.

On a more direct sensory level, possession and addiction are similar because both involve uncontrollable action and reaction of the victim. An addict loses self-control, loses the virtue of mastering his sensual desires and is intensively subjected into satisfying his craving for the addictive substance. It is not just on a substance but any overindulgence in materialistic pleasure could be seen as addiction. This is because any excessive craving for materialism automatically leads to evil manifestations which to these extent demons merge and fulfill their cravings with the affected person. At a personal level, the addict dedicates some or all of his attention, time and personal resources towards obtaining that to which he is addicted; his loved ones also suffer the trauma from this negative ripple effect. At societal level, it drains a nation, reducing its effectiveness and burdening it with extra costs.

Many Christians do not understand that addiction comes from any excessive craving for life fulfillment. Whenever we are unable to say no to gratification, we have an addiction. To avoid bankruptcy, most have made their jobs more important than God, family and health. Some are driving themselves beyond exhaustion to get more money so they can buy more things or live up to an expected luxurious standard. They simply have forgotten that the love for money is the major open door for demonic influences; for any excessive craving for material wealth will definitely lead one into lust, envy, false comfort,idolatry,self ishness,uncompassion,greed,jealousy,thievery,hopelessness,unrep entant sin, despair, no sense of right or wrong, preoccupation to money and eternal death. Anything that has power over you can be used to pry open the door of your heart to satanic influences.

What are the areas that you have been indulging yourself lately? When our flesh is allowed to rule our actions and thoughts, what fruit is produced? (Romans 8:5-11). There are some ways that you can begin to exercise restraint in your affected areas. Let us consider remedies to the common addictive habits in our days; which includes drunkenness, smoking, pornography, drugs, masturbation, promiscuity, gambling (casino, pool and lottery), food, movies, shopping and internet games to mention but a few.

ALCOHOL ADDICTION

Alcoholism is the popular term for alcohol abuse and alcohol dependence. It is a compulsive need for an intoxicating liquid that is obtained from fermented grain or fruit which could be in the form of beer, wine or other hard liquors. The prize of over-indulgence ranges from a hangover to cirrhosis. Alcoholism can lead people into serious trouble because it is physically and mentally destructive. Currently alcohol use is involved in half of all crimes, murders, accidental deaths, and suicides. There are also many health problems associated with alcohol use such as brain damage, cancer, heart disease, and diseases of the liver. More terribly, alcoholics who do not stop drinking reduce life expectancy by 10 to 15 years. Alcoholic hepatitis -inflammation of the liver- and jaundice -a disease which causes yellowness of the skin- due to liver failure are also consequences of heavy drinking. The brain can also be affected by heavy drinking since brain cells are literally destroyed by alcohol. Impaired brain function leads to depression, anxiety, lapse of memory - not mention the more serious brain disorders of dementia, epilepsy and hallucinations.

The pancreas may become inflamed and this lowers blood sugar levels so that the heavy drinker feels tired and drained. Any disturbance in the metabolic processes leads to malnutrition, as damage to the digestive tract interferes with the body's ability to absorb nutrients. As alcoholics consume more alcohol than food, there are deficiencies in some essential nutrients, in particular the B vitamins. The cell regeneration will be affected, thus making the alcoholics much more prone to heart attacks and abnormal heart rhythms because the strength and contraction of the heart muscle is affected by alcohol.

Circulation is damaged, showing itself by numbness or tingling in the fingers. The impaired blood circulation increases the risk of a stroke, a sudden attack that causes unconsciousness and is often followed by paralysis or loss of feeling in the body. Therefore, having known all these deadly effects of alcoholism, yet many Christians do not see drinking as a sin. Someone said, "I am a Christian and I do not see anything wrong with drinking because the Bible did not condemn it.

However I know that drinking to the point of intoxication is strictly forbidden by God, therefore I drink responsibly." Dear friend, I am very sure the same Bible tells us to abstain from all appearances of evil. We should be our brothers' keeper as Paul said in Romans 14:21, "It is good neither to eat flesh, nor to drink wine, nor any thing whereby thy brother stumbleth, or is offended, or is made weak." In the book of 1 Corinthians 8:11-13 he said, "And through thy knowledge shall the weak brother perish, for whom Christ died?

But when ye sin so against the brethren, and wound their weak conscience, ye sin against Christ. Wherefore, if meat makes my brother to offend, I will eat no flesh while the world standeth, lest I make my brother to offend". Whatsoever we do as Christian, we should consider asking ourselves these questions:

1. Will this act causes the weak in the faith confused and doubtful about our belief? 2. How will the unbelievers see me? 3. What example am I setting for my children?

If someone sees a Pastor at a restaurant with a glass of wine in his hand, do they know whether that is his first glass or tenth? All they see is a Pastor drinking an alcoholic beverage. What impression does this creates in their mind? Clear enough, no one wanted to be an alcoholic, it all started with a sip. Therefore brethren, night is far spent, the day is at hand: let us therefore cast off the works of darkness, and let us put on the armor of light. Let us walk honestly, as in the day; not in rioting and drunkenness, not in chambering and wantonness, not in strife and envying, we should put on our Lord Jesus Christ and make no provision for the flesh, to fulfill the lusts thereof. For it is not for Kings to drink wine; nor for Prince strong drink: lest they drink, forget the law, and pervert the judgment of any of the afflicted. We are peculiar people, a royal priesthood, therefore be not among the winebibbers, among the gluttonous eaters of flesh: for the drunkard and the glutton shall come to poverty and drowsiness will clothe a man with rags. **Drunkenness leads to poverty**: A chronic drunk rarely provide for his family. All his monthly earnings ends up in the bar and women. This is not a life worthy of a Christian because a man who cannot provide for his family is worst than an infidel. Proverbs 21:17 He that loves pleasure shall be a poor man: he that loves wine and oil shall not be rich. Proverbs 23:21 for the drunkard and the glutton shall come to poverty: and drowsiness shall clothe a man with rags.

It leads to strife, woe and sorrow: Proverbs 23:29-30 who hath woe? Who hath sorrow? Who hath contentions? Who hath babbling? Who hath wounds without cause? Who hath redness of eyes? They that tarry long at the wine; they that go to seek mixed wine.

It brings error, scorning and contempt to God's work: Isaiah 28:7 But they also have erred through wine, and through strong drink are out of the way; the priest and the prophet have erred through strong drink, they are swallowed up of wine, they are out of the way through strong drink; they err in vision, they stumble in judgment. Isaiah 5:12 and the harp, and the viol, the tabret, and pipe, and wine, are in their feasts: but they regard not the work of the LORD, neither consider the operation of his hands. Hosea 7:5 In the day of our king the princes have made him sick with bottles of wine; he stretched out his hand with scorners.

It overcharge the heart, brings rioting and wantonness : The book of Luke 21:34 tells us to take heed to yourselves, lest at any time your hearts be overcharged with surfeiting, and drunkenness, and cares of this life, and so that day come upon you unawares. Romans 13:13… let us walk honestly, as in the day; not in rioting and drunkenness, not in chambering and wantonness, not in strife and envying. Therefore, the Bible admonished us in Ephesians 5:18 not to be drunk with wine, wherein is excess; but be filled with the Spirit; Luke 21:34 said … take heed to yourselves, lest at any time your hearts be overcharged with surfeiting, and drunkenness, and cares of this life, and so that day come upon you unawares. Galatians 5:21 declared…envying, murders, drunkenness, reveling, and such like: of which I tell you before, as I have also told you in time past, that they which do such things shall not inherit the kingdom of God. Drinking or drunkenness is a proximate cause that set in motion train of sinfulness, a promo of the demons.

How to Stop Alcoholism

Some may think that it's just a matter of having the will to stop drinking, but alcoholism is more complicated than that. An alcoholic's craving for alcohol is so great that it suppresses their ability to stop drinking. The majority of alcoholics need assistance to stop drinking. With treatment and support from family and friends, many have been able to stop drinking and rebuild their lives. It is a sad fact that there are still some who are unable to stop in spite of these aids.

Firstly, you must have a serious desire to quit alcoholism. Have the initiative to identify the cause of your being alcoholic. Knowing the cause of one problem is an important part to its solution. If being alcoholic is due to some traumatic experiences, you must let go and be delivered from it. Forgiveness is a good thing to do. Seek counseling to aid in healing. Make the decision to get help. Recognizing the need for help is one important thing to do. There are a lot of alcohol rehabilitation centers that could give you assistance for your treatment. You can also get different kinds of help from your family, friends, and above all from God.

SMOKING

Burning tobacco originated with ancient aboriginals. The modern world learned of the use of tobacco from the Indians. History reveals Columbus found the Indians smoking and watched with surprise and wonderment. The Grand Pipe or Pipe of Peace was first observed among the Indians of Upper Mississippi country by the French. They called these pipes "calumets". According to the Indians the pipe possessed a supernatural power and a "charming" effect to compel the partakers of the smoke to a brotherly bond of peace (obviously not the peace of the Lord Jesus Christ). Historically the calumet was considered a sacred pipe to offer smoke to the demon gods above and below. Tobacco was looked upon as a sacred plant and burning it brought favor in the eyes of the gods (demons).

Even a member of an enemy tribe who entered a house and smoked with the host, was guaranteed protection and safe conduct when he left. Several Indian tribes burned incense for a purifying medium or an acceptable offering to the unseen. Some eastern tribes did not smoke a pipe in a sacred ceremony but burned tobacco in a small fire. This smoke offering was believed to ascend to the power to whom they prayed. As the use of tobacco as an offering to gods continued, it was rolled in corn husks, the predecessors of modern cigars and cigarettes. Inhaling the smoke was incorporated into the rituals and both the smoke and the aroma continued to have a serious place in the religious rituals and ceremonies. History reference books also state the tobacco pipe was used by American Indians in ceremonies to ratify treaties.

Also, some Indians smoked the tobacco pipes to their sun-god and blew the smoke to him. Indians related many sources of illnesses to "witches who flew through the air disguised as owls to poison their victims". The protective practice against these witches was to cut their limbs and cleanse themselves of bad blood; and the use of "the old man's tobacco" was to avert spirits of the dead.

Smoking is a psychological, emotional and physical addiction that destroys your body. Despite the sickness and disease associated with this smoking ranging from

{a}lung cancer,{b}cancer of the mouth, {c}cancer of the throat , {d}cancer of the larynx {e}cancer of the esophagus, {f}stomach cancer , {g}kidney cancer , {h}cancer of the bladder {i}cancer of the pancreas, {j}liver cancer, {k}cancer of the penis , {l}cancer of the anus {m}cervical cancer , {n}prostate cancer, {o}heart attack

, {q}coronary heart disease cardiovascular disease, {r}congestive heart failure, {s}stroke , {t}atherosclerosis , {u}abdominal aortic aneurysm to asthma , {v}diabetes, {w}stomach ulcers, {x}cataracts, gum disease, high blood pressure ,Crohn's disease, to premature aging of the skin as clearly stipulated by health specialist, millions still indulge in this habit.

Crohn's disease is also known as granulomatous colitis and regional enteritis, an inflammatory disease of the digestive system which may affect any part of the gastrointestinal tract from the mouth to anus. Smoking harms others. For the Christian it is to be specially noted that the smoker forces all these above mentioned plagues, diseases and problems on other innocent people in the smoker's presence. Co-workers, family and especially children are victims of the smoke from the smoker and cigarettes. Christians are definitely not to be stumbling blocks to others. Think how God views it when a believer, by smoking causes others, especially children, to endure burning eyes, clogged nasal passages, undue colds, flu, nervous disorders and hindrances to mind function! Even asthma and cancers!

Yes, Christian smoker - You are guilty of these! Others are offended by a smoking believer yet most endure the offense silently. The children and infants tormented by tobacco smoke have no choice but to endure silently. II Corinthians 6:3 is a command to followers of Christ to "give no offense in anything, that the ministry be not blamed". Serious and sobering warning from the Lord Jesus himself concerning our offending others, especially children (smoking Christian parents take special note), is written in Matthew 18: 6, 7, "But who so shall offend one of these little ones which believe in me, it were better for him that a millstone were hanged about his neck, and that he were drowned in the depths of the sea. Woe unto the world because of offenses! For it must needs be that offenses come; but woe to that man by whom the offense cometh!" We have seen above that the smoker not only smokes but buys misery, destruction and death.

So why do people smoke? Most people smoke in order to cope with stress or nerves, others because of peer pressure and influence while many says it relaxes them, helps them to concentrate, reduces tension, stress, anger and makes it easier to make friends. A lot of people do it out of habit and they don't even really want a cigarette some of the time. This means that smoking has taken the place of the Holy Spirit in man but God forbid.

No, reason whatsoever is justifiable to destroy the temple of God. "Don't you know that your body is the temple of the Holy Spirit, who lives in you and was given to you by God? You do not belong to yourself, for God bought you with a high price. So you must honor God with your body." Christians desire to be seen of the Lord as "good stewards". How much financial resource is "going up in smoke" from believer-smokers?

What would Jesus say about this waste of funds that otherwise could go to evangelism, missionary work or the needy? Should a smoking believer even pray for God's financial blessings? Most probably the smoking believer causes a curse to come upon his or her finances. Though the bible did not outstandingly condemn it but the act of destroying your body makes it a sin, hurts your testimony and controls you. Satan and the unclean spirits (demons) know they have spiritual "legal right or ground" to successfully attack and harm (steal, kill, destroy) the smoking believer!

Spiritually speaking (the way God sees it) cigarette smoking is "burning incense to other (demon) gods". II Kings 22:17, II Kings 23:5; II Chronicles 28:25, 34:24-25; Jeremiah 1:16, 7:9,11:12, 19:4.

How to Stop Smoking

1. Make up your mind: it takes a strong, concrete and irreversible determination to stop. See the reasons why you must stop:

- You are prone to dying young.
- You would not want your children to smoke.
- You must gain control over your life.

- You cannot live longer and healthier.
- You can buy a new car from the money you saved.
- You will want to smell good at all time and avoid the risk of fire.
- keep the body Holy for God

2. Ask Jesus to help you. He is able, abundantly able to deliver and to save anyone the trust in him. John 1:9 tells us: "If we confess our sins, he is faithful and just o forgive us our sins, and to cleanse us from all unrighteousness. For as many that receive Him, He gave the power to become the sons of God. He is greater than the urge for smoking and has given you the power to overcome this temptation, all you need is just have faith in him.

3. Quit all your smoking friends. It does not mean they are your enemies but reduce regular visitation or outing with them rather spend your leisure with non-smokers.

4. Reject every offer of cigarette and leave the scene as soon as possible.

5. Read your bible or any other scriptural material whenever you are sad, angry or depressed. Recitation of a pre-chosen scriptural verse will help.

6. Out loudly rebuke the urge whenever it comes. The name Jesus overpowers every urge, desire and lust in man, His grace shall be with you for eternity.

PORNOGRAPHY

Looking at degrading pictures of naked women and men, reading tales of sexual adventure or watching videos of fornication are all compulsive habits that have ruined many lives including Christians. Any image, picture, statue, advertisement or write up, whose purpose is to sexually titillate is pornography. Even the media and advertisement firms are using the exploitation of the body more blatantly than ever before. Intimate physical details are no longer being airbrushed out of photographed models; such details are even being drawn in on newsprint ad models just for attraction. Many men report using these same pictures as stimuli for their masturbation fantasies.

Pornography according to 1986 Attorney General Commission on Pornography is defined as predominantly sexually explicit, intended primarily for the purpose of sexual arousal. It is a sexual explicit in the extreme, and devoid of any other apparent content or purpose. It distorts God's gift of sex, which should only be shared in marriage. It defiles and causes the mind to wander in wanton lustful imagination. Pornography is promoted in many ways:

- Adult magazines, which are primarily directed toward adult male readers.
- Video cassettes and CD.
- Motion pictures.
- Television.
- Audio Porn.
- The Internet or Cyber porn. Almost anyone can download and view hard-core pictures, movies, online chat, and even live sex acts through the internet.

Verbal conversations. This is common among peers or schoolmates. Boys and girls of the same interest sit together to share their sexual experiences. Teaching the innocent ones on what and what not to do about men, women and sex, also do women share their sexual experience with their friends; these are all forms of oral pornography. All these mediums aimed at promoting lustful desire and igniting sexual gratification within humanity.

These images or stories of people who are engaged in sexual activity, are specifically designed to make people lust, so its existence or participation is a sin Matthew 5:28. Every porn addict is prone to sexual sin, sexual imagination and lustful desires. It directly controls the mind of the addict into all assorts of sexual imagination, jokes, speeches and actions. The Bible warns that let no corrupt communication proceed out of our mouth, but that which is good to the use of edification, that it may minister grace unto the hearers. And grieve not the Holy Spirit of God, whereby ye are sealed unto the day of redemption. Ephesians 4:29-30.

The true Christian should be sexually pure, so we should guide our minds against lustful imagination and sin. In viewing pornography, nakedness or any sexual displays lust is not only given the opportunity to rise but most often lustful passions and thoughts are triggered in the heart and mind thus yielding to sin. In Matt 5:27, Jesus declared" You have heard that it was said ,you shall not commit adultery; but I say to you, that everyone who looks on a woman to lust for her has committed adultery with her already in his heart."

Apostle Paul advised us to flee immorality. Every other sin that a man commits is outside the body, but the immoral man sins against his own body." Therefore consider the members of your earthly body as dead to immorality, impurity, passion, evil desire, and greed, which amount to idolatry."Col 3:5, Habakkuk 2:15 declared woe to him who gives drink to his neighbors, pouring it from the wineskin till they are drunk, so that he can gaze on their naked bodies" Meats for the belly, and the belly for meats: but God shall destroy both it and them, for your body is not for fornication, but for the Lord; and the Lord for the body says 1 Corinthians 6:13. The fruits of pornography are all sinful which includes, masturbation, sexual exposure (Gen. 9:21-23), adultery (Lev. 18:20), bestiality (Lev. 18:23), homosexuality (Lev. 18:22 and 20:13), incest (Lev. 18:6-18), and prostitution (Deut. 23:17- 18).

Therefore you should set no unclean thing before your eyes. Keep your hearts and minds in Christ Jesus...for whatsoever things are pure... if there be any virtues... think on these things. Psalm 101:3, Philippians 4:7, 8.

How to stop Pornographic Addiction

Pornography like all other addictions has a strong drive for continuity. You only need a concrete decision and determination to stop this act. You have to believe in Jesus; in Him only you will have the ability to take captive every thought to make it obedient to Christ. He will give you the ability to cancel out every impure thought and imagination, making you victorious over the enemy on a regular daily basis.

1. Determination. Porn addiction like every other compulsive addiction needs your determination to stop. Determination is the starting point of all achievement, not a hope, not a wish, but a keen pulsating desire which transcends everything. Without a strong determination, your desire for a new life will be half-hearted and produce little results. A strong determination considers nothing but the goal that is ahead until achievement is made there is no rest.

As an act built in the mind but manifests in the flesh, it is still within your will to control. See it as an enemy that robs you of your intimacy and inheritance with God, it is a bait of the devil to lure many into all sorts of sexual immorality. God in His holiness wants us to live a sinless life, a true grace filled life that men will see your good works and glorify Him the Father. Therefore, Let not sin reign in your mortal body, that ye should obey it in the lusts thereof. Neither yields you your members as instruments of unrighteousness unto sin: but yield yourselves unto God, as those that are alive from the dead, and your members as instruments of righteousness unto God. For sin shall not have dominion over you: for ye are not under the law, but under grace. What then? Shall we sin, because we are not under the law, but under grace? God forbid. Know ye not, that to whom ye yield yourselves servants to obey, his servants ye are to whom ye obey; whether of sin unto death, or of obedience unto righteousness? But God be thanked, that ye were the servants of sin, but ye have obeyed from the heart that form of doctrine which was delivered you.

Being then made free from sin, ye became the servants of righteousness. Romans 6:12-18.

2. Pray and confess your sin to God. Repentance involves the following, seeing your sin-1 John 1:8, 10, sorrowing over your sin. You must do more than admitting your sin, rather internally engage with it. Psalm 51:17; Isaiah 57:15; 2 Corinthians 7:9. You must confess the sin. We must put our sin into words and agree with God that what we did was wrong. Psalm 51:4; Hosea 14:1-3; 2 Corinthians 7:11; 1 John 1:9. You must be ashamed of your sin, hate your sin.

Finally, you must turn away from your sin and bear the fruit of repentance. Matthew 3:7-8; Acts 26:20. Godly sorrow brings repentance that leads to salvation and leaves no regret" (2 Corinthians 7:10). Repent of your sin and ask Jesus to come into your heart, to cleanse and deliver you from this evil. No sin is too black or wicked that the blood of Jesus cannot cleanse you from it. The book of 1 John 1:9-10, and 2:1-2 reminded us that "If we confess our sins, he is faithful and just to forgive us our sins, and to cleanse us from all unrighteousness. If we say that we have not sinned, we make him a liar, and his word is not in us. My little children, these things write I unto you, that ye sin not. And if any man sin, we have an advocate with the Father, Jesus Christ the righteous: And he is the propitiation for our sins: and not for ours only, but also for the sins of the whole world."

3. Pornography opens you up to demonic control and manifestation; therefore, you need   someone who has the gift of the Holy Spirit to pray deliverance over you. You should seek for a Bible believing church that knows how to deal with demons. The Lord will lead you in this matter if you ask Him. Do not allow pride to prevent you from getting help and getting free if you need it. James 4:7-8, "Submit yourselves therefore to God. Resist the devil, and he will flee from you. Draw nigh to God, and he will draw nigh to

you. Cleanse your hands, ye sinners; and purify your hearts, ye double minded."

4. Live a committed Christian life. Get involved in as many church activities as possible, this will help set your mind on things that above where Christ sits on the throne. As you commit your life to Christ in total obedience and submission, your victory is assured. A life of holiness is the only true victorious life.

5. You must stay away from its areas of temptation and destroy all videos, games, magazines that relates to pornography. If you must use the computer in your work environment, you should employ a filter service for your ISP or software that filters out those evil invitations so they do not enter your e-mail and cannot be accessed by your browser. 1 Corinthians 6:18-20 advised us to "Flee fornication. Every sin that a man doeth is without the body; but he that committed fornication sinned against his own body. Know ye not that your body is the temple of the Holy Ghost which is in you, which ye have of God, and ye are not your own. For ye are bought with a price: therefore glorify God in your body, and in your spirit, which are God's."

6. Should you stumble or fall, do not stay down. Do not be discourage Just ask the Lord to forgive you and start again in your walk with Him. Ask Him to empower you to overcome. You cannot do it in your strength. Just remember that in Him you can do all things. Philippians 4:13: "I can do all things through Christ which strengthened me."

7. A lonely mind is the devil's workshop. This urge seems to overshadow your will when you are lonely, therefore get involve in some activities. This battle is staged in the mind. Therefore, you must cast down every imagination that do not agree with the Bible and quote the Word of God over your body and mind. 2 Corinthians 10:3-5 "For though we walk in the flesh, we do not war after the flesh: (For the weapons of our warfare are not carnal,

but mighty through God to the pulling down of strong holds;) casting down imaginations, and every high thing that exalted itself against the knowledge of God, and bringing into captivity every thought to the obedience of Christ."

8. Avoid friends who discuss filthy things. Let your companion be with brethrens who shares the word edifying each other in holiness.

9. Have the home computer in a public place

10. Frequently check the computer for spyware/adware/malware by installing an anti-spyware program. Many do not know that porn sites routinely place this stuff into computers.

11. Use a password system so that children cannot be on the computer by themselves.

12. be careful of what gets watched on TV .Any partial nudity and sex scenes could certainly trigger a desire to return to porn. Also make sure that magazines with sexual stories and partial nudity are not in the house

13. Parents must teach their children a biblical view of sex and the consequences that befalls sinners.

14. Commit a life of prayer. The grace of God which passes all understanding will be with you.

15. When dealing with pornography, it is a decision that often must be made continuously. Don't stop repenting even if it is the 1000 and more time.

MASTURBATION

It is self-stimulation to cause sexual sensations, which requires the essential elements of thoughts and fantasy to bring gratification and release to the person. Every other thought are subdued to heighten imaginations during the act, in the man, it is orgasmic in nature with ejaculation while in the woman, her release is orgasmic. This compulsive, defiling and addictive habit is called self-abuse, solo-sex, self-love, or self-gratification.

Most people visualize wild sexual fantasies or use hard pornography, photographs or sexually suggestive stories to heighten the pleasure but all of these are, in reality form of mind idolatry involving the worship of another person, the worship of sex itself, or the worship of an image,--rather than God. As Men are more easily visually stimulated, so are women vulnerable to sexual fantasy in the emotional realm but every sexual immorality begins with a thought and it is sin in God's eyes. This addiction increases everyday as this demon gains control over the mind narrowing it towards doing the act often.

Masturbation defiles the mind and emission of semen is an abomination before God. The Bible is clear that sexual activity is always wrong outside of marriage hence masturbation can never be fulfilling and satisfying since it is inherently an incomplete act to which there is no response or appropriate answerback from a complementary partner, it will rather turn one's focus inward upon oneself. The Bible declares, "I made a covenant with my eyes not to look with lust upon a girl. I know fully well that the Almighty God sends calamity on those who do" (Job 31:1-3). You have heard that it was said, 'Do not commit adultery.' But I tell you that anyone who looks at a woman lustfully has already committed adultery with her in his heart" (Matthew 5:28).

Masturbation brings guilt, shame and fear of being found out. It reduced psychological creative energy, lessens interest in interpersonal relationships, lowers self-esteem and increases self-consciousness, destroys your health as it can cause fatigue and tiredness all the time, lower back pain, stress and anxiety, thinning hair/hair loss, soft/weak erection, premature ejaculation, eye floater/fuzzy vision, testicular pain and low memory capacity. It prevents you from having better sex with your partner, makes you spend most of your valuable time watching pornographic content, prevents you from making your life's dream come true, successful people are not addicted to the habit of masturbation simply because they spend their time doing what is important for them and their loved ones and not in masturbation

Most parents are carefree about the activities of their grown up children. From the stage of puberty until marriage, do you really care about the sexual feelings of your children? The sermons and bible classes are not enough because there are some questions I will prefer to ask my folks at home and not in the church. The norms of God's word designates that we benefit ourselves by strongly resisting all unchaste habits in act, word, thought and all inordinate affections, putting to death therefore your members which are upon the earth: fornication, uncleanness, passion, evil desires as regards sexual appetite. (Colossians 3:5)

Masturbation also installs certain attitudes that are mentally corrupting because when masturbating, a person is immersed in his or her own bodily sensations, very self-centered. (See 2 Corinthians 11:3.) Sex becomes separated from love and is relegated to a reflex that releases tension. Nevertheless, God intended that sexual desires be satisfied in sexual relations; an expression of love between a man and his wife. Proverbs 5:15-19. Since this act requires lustful imaginations, irrespective of the justifying argument by any authority I wish to strongly admonish fellow Christians to abstain from this act for God frowns at it.

Remember that emission of semen is a sin. "When a man has emission of semen, he must bathe his whole body with water and he will be unclean till evening".......when a man lies with a woman and there is an emission of semen, both must bathe with water and they will be unclean till evening"...Leviticus 15:16 and 18. Therefore, since Christ suffered in his body, arm yourselves also with the same attitude, because he who has suffered in his body is done with sin. As a result, he does not entangle his earthly life for evil human desires, but rather for the will of God. As the book of

Galatians 5 verses 24 said … those who are Christ's have crucified the flesh with its passions and desires. I Peter 2:11 Beloved, I beg you as sojourners and pilgrims, abstain from fleshly lusts which war against the soul.

How to control Masturbation

Determination is the first step to salvage your addiction. You must decide that you will end this practice, and when you make that decision, the problem will be greatly reduced at once. Pray, asking God for forgiveness and power to overcome this instinct. Then observe the following:

1. Do not touch or play with your genital organ except during the normal call of nature.

2. Avoid loneliness as much as possible. Find good friends and stay with them. Loneliness and depression are two powerful factors that cause masturbation in both men and women.

3. Do not associate with people having this same weakness. Being in their presence will keep this problem in your mind.

4. Avoid staying in the bathe room longer and do not admire yourself in a mirror.

5. If your problem is normally during the bedtime, dress yourself securely that you cannot touch your genital organ.

6. If the urge seems to be overpowering you, get out of the bed and fix yourself into some activities outside.
    Pick your phone and call a good friend, this is just to get your mind on something else.

7. Avoid reading pornographic material, erotic write ups or any material that deals with nudity. Avoid people, situations, pictures or reading materials that might create sexual excitement.

8. Put wholesome thoughts into your mind all the time. Engage in reading Christian books, Bible or any material that edifies.

9. Commit into prayers. Let your inner man understand that you are the temple of God. Do not pray about this problem because that will keep it in your mind. Rather pray for faith and understanding, I tell you, any form of scriptural practice puts the devil on a run.

10. The gift of the Spirit will give you more strength for your daily victory. Pray for this gift.

11. When the urge is strong on you, out loudly reject it in the name of Jesus Christ, recite a verse in the Bible or sing inspirational praise to God. You will be surprise how this works.

12. Engage yourself in exercise that will reduce emotional tension and depression.

13. Try to overcome this act for a day, and then a week, a month, a year then you will never do it again.

14. Be friendly and outgoing, try to be with others and enjoy a good social outing.

15. Take a cool shower but remembers to leave your door or curtain partly opens to discourage being alone. Satan never gives up but you are more than conquerors in the name of Jesus Christ.

16. Engage in body exercise whenever you are idle.

GAMBLING/CASINO ADDICTION

"Slaves who love their chains can never be free".

Firstly, let us consider some Biblical examples of gambling: Samson wagered 30 linen garments and sets of clothes with the Philistines to see if they could guess his riddle, but due to

Philistine pressure on his bride, he lost the bet and in anger he struck down 30 other Philistines in Ashkelon to pay off the debt, Judges 14:12-19. The garments of our Messiah were parted by lot, Psalm 22:18, Matthew 27:35, Luke 23:34, John 19:23-24. Haman, the enemy of the Jews, cast lots to fix the time of execution of the Jews, Esther 3:7, 9:24. The enemies of Judah and Jerusalem cast lots for God's people, Joel 3:3, Obadiah 11. These are instances of the wrong use of gambling/bet in the bible. There are also many Scriptural examples of the correct use of lot/gambling to determine God's will, and it was a priest, prophet, apostle or other representative of the Eternal who was authorized to use this method of discerning God's will. The scapegoat was chosen by lot, Leviticus 16:8-10. The land of Canaan was divided among the tribes by lot, Numbers 26:55, Joshua 18:10, Acts 13:19, Isaiah 34:17.

The garments of Aaron were passed on to his son Eleazar, Numbers 20:28. Achan's guilt was determined by lot, Joshua 7:14-18. Saul was chosen king by lot, 1 Samuel 10:20-21. The order of service by priests and Levites was determined by lot, 1 Chronicles 24:5-31, 26:13. Jonathan was identified by lot, I Samuel 14:41-42. So was Jonah, Jonah 1:7. The Jews returning from captivity determined by lot who would live in Jerusalem, Nehemiah 11:1. The eleven apostles cast lots between two candidates to allow God to decide who should replace Judas Iscariot, Acts 1:26.

Casino Today

Everything might be going on perfectly in your life, good job, happy family, successful life and friends until the day you stepped into the casino. By the time you realized it 5 to 8 years of your life is gone without any basic achievement, just like a man under the influence of a love portion, you will be spiritually bewitched. The memories of your previous financial buoyancy before the struck of your present dilemma will keep you depressed and sad at all time. You cannot tell anybody what you are going through for fear of gossips or been called names.

I advised myself not to be involved in any form of gambling or casino, said Robert. The $2900 profit I had earlier today turned into a $4500 loss because I lacked self-control. I do not even know how it happened, he lamented. Casino or gambling is like the cancer of the liver, it eats you up gradually. It is a degenerating time wasting hobby that perpetuates the idea that money can buy you happiness or that money can buy money without hard work. These are common helpless and hopeless expression of a chronic gambler:

- I wish I had quit while I was ahead.
- Oh! Nearly
- Another trial will hit it big!

Unfortunately, casino takes all your money, wastes your precious time in life and leaves you feeling like crap. It is so dangerous that it makes you forget how dejected, depressed, lonely, helpless and hopeless you felt the last time you lost money, rather it gives you a fake confidence to try again with the hope of recovering your lost. I am sorry if this offends anyone but I hope after reading passage all of you can find the strength to walk away and get your lives back. Though not everyone loses money, but I am very sure that 90% of gamblers lose more money than they will like to lose. Each time the gamblers win a little money, it excites them because the fact that they won little money drives them on.

They always tell themselves, one more try at the slot machines. But like the bite of a little mouse on the foot of a sleeper, the casinos enable them to keep gambling by offering them free drinks and live music in the hopes that they will spend more money at the casino. Up till now all your hopes may have been dependent on that very big win. If you stop gambling you may believe that all your dreams of getting that big win is being taken away, however if you continue to gamble your debts will increase as your life deteriorate.

Regrettably, you cannot get back the money you have lost, the more you play to recover your money, the more you lose the ones in your wallet; just like the more you look the less you see. You even might have budgeted how you will manage the big win when it comes but it is just mere daydreaming! It can never come to reality. Until the last dollar in your wallet is gone, you will never realize how miserable you are, a walking corpse heading to cemetery. Basically, you are becoming irresponsible to yourself, family and society. That many committed suicide because they lost lots of money in casino does not sound as a note of warning to a chronic gambler simply because the demon of casino is a strong and deceitful one. It lures and controls the mind of an addict into playing more with the hope of winning at the next turn; the more you play, the more committed you become and the more you lose.

However, many could see it as a moral choice but in actual sense it is very difficult for this addict to give up his habit because he has lost control of his mind and body, save for divine grace that restores. Though Bible does not directly prohibit gambling or casino as some may say but following its principles and example, a true Christian will clearly rule it out as a sin. Casino or gambling is sin because it is motivated by greed and covetousness as the aim of the every gambler is to get lots of money quickly! The scripture condemns greed and covetousness. Thou shall not covet... is the tenth commandment. Three passages show that God hates and will not save a covetous man. Psalm 10:3: "For the wicked boasted of his heart's desire, and blessed the covetous, whom the Lord hateth." I Corinthians 6:9, 10: "Know ye not that the unrighteous shall not inherit the kingdom of God? Be not deceived: neither ... thieves, nor covetous ... shall inherit the kingdom of God."Ephesians 5:5: "For this ye know, that no ... covetous man, who is an idolater, hath any inheritance in the kingdom of God and of Christ."

Paul said, in the name of the Lord Jesus Christ, we command you, brothers, to keep away from every brother who is idle and does not live according to the teaching you received from us. For you know how you ought to follow our example. We were not idle when we were with you, nor did we eat anyone's food without paying for it. On the contrary, we worked night and day, laboring and toiling so that we would not be a burden to any of you. We did this, not because we do not have the right to such help, but in order to make ourselves a model for you to follow. For even when we were with you, we gave you this rule: "If a man will not work, he shall not eat." We hear that some among you are idle. They are not busy; they are busybodies. Such people we command and urge in the Lord Jesus Christ to settle down and earn the bread they eat. And as for you, brothers, never tire of doing what is right. In Second Thessalonians 3:6-13, Paul also warned against covetousness in I Timothy 6:9-10: "but they that will be rich fall into temptation and a snare, and into many foolish and hurtful lusts, which drown men in destruction and perdition.

For the love of money is the root of all evil: which while some coveted after, they have erred from the faith, and pierced themselves through with many sorrows." The writer to the Hebrews said: "Let your conversation be without covetousness; and be content with such things as ye have; for he hath said, I will never leave thee, nor forsake thee" (13:5).

Gambling or casino is a sin because:

- It discourages honest labor and promotes laziness. Proverbs 14:23; in all labor there is profit, but idle talk leads only to poverty." Profit should come through productive labor, not by chance. "Wealth not earned but won in haste, or unjustly, or from the production of things for vain or detrimental use, such riches will dwindle away; but he who gathers little by little will increase them" Proverbs 13:11. See also Proverbs 28:19. It encourages greed, materialism and discontent. See Luke 12:15, Hebrews 13:5, I Timothy 6:6-10, Psalm 62:10. Lottery promotions induce people to covet the money of others.

- Gambling such as lotteries are engaged in by people hoping to win a lot of money without earning it, which is a dishonest attitude. Money won in gambling comes from other players, including some who can ill afford to gamble.

- Gambling in its essence is a form of robbery, which is stealing. Each gambler wants to get the prize money for himself.

- It encourages greedy obsession with material wealth, which is having another god in place of the true Creator.

- Gambling directly breaks the first, eighth and tenth commandments, and all the others in principle.

- John 2:15-17 says, "Love not the world neither the things that are in the world. If any man loves the world, the love of the Father is not in him. For all that is in the world, the lust of the flesh, and the lust of the eyes, and the pride of life, is not of the Father, but is of the world. And the world passeth away, and the lust thereof: but he that doeth the will of God abideth for ever." Proverbs 21:25-26, "The desire of the slothful killeth him; for his hands refuse to labour. He coveteth greedily all the day long: but the righteous giveth and spareth not."

- It is a "get rich quick" syndrome.

- See Proverbs 28:20, 22; 21:5. Proverbs 23:4-5, "Labour not to be rich: cease from thine own wisdom. Wilt thou set thine eyes upon that which is not, for riches certainly makes themselves wings; they fly away as an eagle toward heaven."

How to stop casino/gambling

When you are enslaved to any behavior especially gambling, the Holy Spirit is not in you and frequently you may encounter all the difficulties stated below because you are no longer able to discern your behavior carefully.

a. You will be filled with stress, worries and anxiety.
b. Everyone around you gets you irritated.
c. You are more secretive
d. You are heavily in debt.
e. You are unable to pay your vows.
f. You are unable to provide for dependent ones.
h. You cannot sleep at night.
i. Soon or later you will beg for food.
j. You are considering suicide now! Please there is a remedy.

Like every other compulsive addictions, you are the answer to you problem. It takes you to solve the problem in you.

The following are the steps you must take to help yourself.

1.Determine in your heart to stop. You are never given a wish, without also being given the power to make it. Determination is the motto of every goal achieved. Therefore make-up your mind and consider your deplorable state. Having made up your mind to stop,

2. Go on your knees and pray to God. Acknowledge and confess your sin before Him, ask Him to give you the strength to carry on. Our almighty Father is so merciful and full in grace as He has promised to purify us when we confess our sins and heal our land. For if we confess our sins, he is faithful and just and will forgive us our sins and purify us from all unrighteousness. (1 John 1:9). And you will have a peace of mind through our Lord Jesus.

3. You must accept that all the money you have lost is gone. Get off your mind from all your lost because any thought of it could possibly push into further trial for recovering. Do you know that many died the very day they entered their new expensive car. Many died the very day they opened their new house. A good

friend of mine died the very day he graduated from school of medicine. Therefore your lost is not an exception rather it is all part of the experiences in life. Forget the lost money and move on.

4. Stay away from any gambling friend. Postpone every appointment with them and do not often answer when they call as they might encourage you to gamble.

5. Keep away from any casino or gambling houses. You could be push to gamble on mere sighting the arena.

6. Do not keep much cash on you. Always limits the amount of money in your home and wallet

7. Get someone you could trust to manage your finance or run the family's finance.

8. Share this problem with your trusted friend, the power of sin lies on exposure. Whenever sin is brought to light, it steam reduces.

9. Read as many rotten write-ups about casino as you can. May the grace of our Lord Jesus Christ be with you.

INTERNET ADDICTION

In this recent time, technology has improved and people have access to the internet. Many go to internet for information, entertainment, relationship, fraud and support. The invention of the internet had made communication much easier, faster and less expensive because it provides the users with website, email, instant communication and marketing. Recent research findings have proved that women are now online more than men,

- 50% of the people online do not tell their exact age, weight, job, marital status and gender.

- 30 % of the people going online will experience clear negative impacts to their life.
- 20 % of the people going online are becoming addicted.

Internet addiction is a contributing factor in nearly 50% of all relationship and family problems. The excessive use of the internet is called net addiction or net junkie. It is a problem because it affects personal behavior, interpersonal relationship or even death. The significant problems of frequent users are

1. Personal neglect.
2. Isolation and avoidance from people.
3. Less productivity.
4. Depression
5. Marital problems.
6. Sexual addiction
7. Pornographic addiction
8. Casino addiction/gambling away savings.
9. Internet abuse
10. Academic failure. A compulsive and potentially addicted user is online for more than 10 hours a day in non-work related activity. He spends more time online, feel better when chatting with opposite sex, can never be industrious and feels like committing suicide whenever there is connection failure. Men dominated the Net until just recently women turned worst. Men seek out pornography while women seeking out relationships. Nevertheless, men and women are using the Internet equally for "cybering" (cyber sex). Cyber sex is defined as the consensual sexual discussion online for the purpose of achieving arousal or an orgasm.

A cyber addicted Christian is likely to be a porn addict, a sex addict or an online casino addict. He expenses less time for the scripture and prayers, even sometimes he doesn't pray at all, as such he needs deliverance. In fact, if you are a passive Christian, you are likely to be an addict and cannot make a good use of your time. Like every other addiction, the internet controls your mind, actions and in such body, the Holy Spirit does not dwell. The addiction has taken the place of the Holy Spirit leaving you empty and prone to the devil but though your condition is deplorable, all hope is not lost yet.

Christ can do it, and He will live in you if you will let Him. Yes, it is still your decision to make, simply ask Jesus for help and believe Him for salvation. This is a temptation but He will not let you be tempted above that which you are able to stand, believe Him. Secondly, disconnect your internet for a while, time yourself and only spend time maybe doing emails. Jesus says if your eye offends you pluck it out for it is better to get into heaven with one eye than cast into hell fire with both, and if your right hand offends you, cut it off, better to go into the kingdom of heaven lame than be cast into hell with both hands.

Get rid of your internet. Make a list each day of the things you need to do and give yourself an allotted time for internet. May the grace of God be with you!

GENERAL DELIVERANCE

Victory over all addictions both the ones mentioned and ones not mentioned is very imperative for the reoccupation of your dominion. The good news is followers and disciples of the Lord Jesus Christ can secure total and complete victory over addictions. For true a Christ-follower the testimony is not, "I'm a recovering addict" but rather Jesus Christ has set me absolutely free of addictions! Total victory over addiction can be achieved through these four aspects: your own will, counseling, deliverance for your soul and physical reinforcement.

1. Your own will. You personally must make a serious commitment to be free. It takes setting your determination to follow through to the Lord's victory. "Slaves who love their chains can never be free". Develop a desire to cooperate with the Holy Spirit as He

personalizes a program for your specific and unique needs. God will enhance your will to do His will. God will not violate your will if you do not desire His will for you. The deliverance for your soul involves replacing wrong thoughts and errors in your mind with truths from God's word which is the Holy Scripture. This usually involves some counseling with a God called pastor or competent Christian worker. Also when our thinking is in agreement with God's Word we are ready for deliverance from unclean spirits in the soul area. The deliverance of Jesus Christ from these unclean spirits is absolutely essential for total freedom from addiction.

If the spirits remain it is highly probable they will pull us back into the addiction. Our deliverance from unclean spirits should be seen as a process over time. Deliverance is usually accomplished in a series of sessions and should be ministered by competent Christian workers under proven mature spiritual supervision. Physical reinforcement: to best bring about total victory over addictions, we need reinforcement for our physical body. To begin with, you are advice to implement a quality vitamin mineral food supplement into our daily diet.

~ 7 ~

Sicknesses and Demons

The ground of all expectations, true foundation of our blessed hope, health and prosperity is in Christ's love towards us, and not our love towards Christ. To look inward to our love towards Christ is painfully unsatisfying but to look outward to Christ's love towards us is peace. We do get sick and the majority of us die from the last physical illness like Prophet Elisha did (2 Kings 13:14).

For the Bible has established that all shall die (Heb. 9:27). Yes, we were converted, renewed, sanctified, purchased with the precious blood of Christ and heirs of His glory; yet we are sick sometimes. Then should we say that sickness is part of our salvation, a sign that God is displeased, a natural call or an attack from our enemy to rob us peace and good health. Does sickness intend to bless or curse us? Though sickness is a curse, or to put it in a more biblical way, a part of the curse that came upon mankind through Adams' failure to obey God, we still must understand that it is not only sickness; aging and physical death are also inevitably attached to this original curse.

Yet, mysteriously, God sometimes uses sickness, aging and death as means to operate the eternal salvation and blessing on His people. It may be also used as a means to bringing closeness to the Lord during our lives or to even have our faith tried or tested,

(Job 2:3-10) as the Bible declared "All things work together for good to those who love God, and are called according to His purpose." "All things are yours,-life, death, things present, or things to come: for you are Christ's; and Christ is God's." Rom. 8:28 and I Corinthians 3:22-23. Blessed, I say again, are those who have learned this! Happy are they who can say, when they are ill, "This is my Father's doing. It must be well." Let us consider the explanations below for a clearer understanding.

SICKNESS AS A NATURAL CALL

Though the skill of doctors may continually discover new remedies, and effect surprising cures. The enforcement of wise sanitary regulations may greatly lower the death rate in a land. But, after all,-whether in healthy or unhealthy environments, in mild climates or in cold,-whether treated by homeopathy or allopathy,-men will sicken and die. The days of our years are three-score years and ten; and if by reason of strength they be four-score years, yet is their strength labor and sorrow; for it is soon cut off, and we fly away Psalm 90:10. That witness is indeed true. It was true 3300 years ago and it is true still.

Sickness is everywhere. In Europe, in Asia, in Africa, in America; in hot and cold countries, in civilized nations and in savage tribes,-men, women, and children sicken and die. There is sickness in all the classes; the grace does not lift a believer above the reach of it. Riches cannot buy exemption from it. Rank and Position will not prevent its assaults. Kings and their subjects, masters and servants, rich men and poor, learned and unlearned, teachers and scholars, doctors and patients, ministers and hearers, all alike go down before this great foe. "The rich man's wealth is his strong city." Prov. 18:11.

The Englishman's house is called his castle; but there are no doors and bars which can keep out disease and death. From the crown of our head to the sole of our foot we are liable to disease. Our capacity of suffering is something fearful to contemplate.

Who can count up the ailments by which our bodily frame may be assailed? Sickness is often one of the most humbling and distressing trials that can come upon man.

It can turn the strongest into a little child, and make him feel-"the grasshopper a burden." Eccles. 12:5. It can unnerve the boldest, and make him tremble at the fall of a pin. We are "fearfully and wonderfully made." Psalm 139:14. The connection between body and mind is curiously close. The influence that some diseases can exercise upon the temper and spirits is immensely great. There are ailments of brain, and liver, and nerves, which can bring down a Solomon in mind to a state little better than that of a babe. He that would know to what depths of humiliation poor man can fall has only to attend for a short time on sick-beds.

Yes the reality that no one reading this book now will be alive to the next 100 years makes it an evitable natural call. Then I ask why do people get sick and die? The only explanation that satisfies me is that which the Bible gives. Something has come into the world which has dethroned man from his original position, and stripped him of his original privileges. Something has come in, which, like a handful of gravel thrown into the midst of machinery, has marred the perfect order of God's creation. And what is that something? I answer, in one word, it is sin. "Sin has entered into the world and death by sin." Rom. 5:12.

Sin is the cause of all the sickness, and disease, and pain, and suffering which prevail on the earth. They all are part of that curse which came into the world when Adam and Eve ate the forbidden fruit and fell. There would have been no sickness, if there had been no fall. There would have been no disease, if there had been no sin. Man has sinned, and therefore man suffers. Adam fell from his first estate, and therefore Adam's children sicken and die. But I thank God for Christ Jesus whom His death has given us hope, eternal hope indeed.

The Bible promises us many things about sickness. It is important to keep in mind that while God may not heal your disease, He can and will heal your spirit. Collect and meditate on the scriptures about healing. Here are a few from the King James Bible: Jeremiah 17:14 heal me, O LORD, and I shall be healed; save me, and I shall be saved: for thou art my praise. 1 Peter 2:24 who his own self bare our sins in his own body on the tree that we, being dead to sins, should live unto righteousness: by whose stripes ye were healed.

SICKNESS, CALL TO A HOLY LIVING

While sickness is not what God wanted for us, He is able to use it for good. Sickness, like grief and suffering tend to draw us nearer to God. We immediately realize our frailty and seek His comfort. Families whose loved one suffers from sickness also draw nearer to God searching for comfort, healing or answers. It is true that God can use all things for good. Romans 8:28 made it clear, we know that all things work together for good to them that love God, to them who are the called according to his purpose. Sickness force people to pray. We pray for healing, relief from pain and for comfort.

Prayer is a powerful thing and we are called to pray for the sick. Is any sick among you? Let him call for the elders of the church; and let them pray over him, anointing him with oil in the name of the Lord: (James 5:14). Sickness of the physical body is the cure for the spiritual body. Through sickness and suffering, we are spiritually strengthened. We learn to turn to God for answers and to meet our needs. Hebrews 2:10 tells us that we are made perfect through suffering. God in His mercy has allowed the sickness to continue in order to heal the greater problem, the sick. More so, God can use sickness to chastise us of our sins {see **"the wrath of God and Evil spirit from God"** for more details}.

Sickness helps to remind men of death. Most people live as if they will never die but sickness help to make men think seriously of God, their souls, and the world to come. Most in their days of health can find no time for such thoughts but a severe disease has sometimes a wonderful power of mustering and rallying these thoughts; bringing them up before the eyes of a man's soul. Even a wicked king like Benhadad, when sick, could think of Elisha 2 Kings 8:8. Even heathen sailors, when death was in sight, were afraid, and "cried every man to his god." Jonah 1:5. Surely anything that helps to make men think is good.

Sickness helps to soften men's hearts, and teach them wisdom. Sickness helps to level and humble us. A sick bed is a mighty tamer of such thoughts as these. It forces on us the mighty truth that we are all poor worms, that we "dwell in houses of clay," and are "crushed before the moth." , and that kings and subjects, masters and servants, rich and poor, are all dying creatures, and will soon stand side by side at the bar of God.

In the sight of the coffin and the grave it is not easy to be proud. Surely anything that teaches that lesson is good. Sickness comes to make us strong, it is only temporary. Christ Himself took our infirmities, and bare our sicknesses (Isaiah 53:3 and Matthew 8:17).The Lord Jesus was a "Man of sorrows, and acquainted with grief" and by his stripes we are healed. Therefore, blessed be God! Christ lives, though we may die. Christ lives, though friends and families are carried to the grave. He lives who abolished death, and brought life and immortality to light by the Gospel. He lives who said, "O death, I will be your plagues: 0 grave, I will be your destruction" (Hosea 13:14).   He lives who will one day change our vile body, and make it like unto His glorious body. In sickness and in health, in life and in death, let us lean confidently on Him. Surely we ought to say daily with one of old, "Blessed be God for Jesus Christ!"

SICKNESS, AN ATTACK FROM SATAN.

Though sickness is not always produced by demons as seem above. Sometimes Satan or demons may even be part of God's plans to afflict us. In reality we may not know how exactly that is, but that is precisely what the Bible teaches. We all know the story of Job, a righteous man more than any other man on earth according to

God Himself. But God allowed Satan to destroy not only Job's possession but also his health to the point of desperation. Job wanted to die. It was a horrible situation and was caused by God (Job 2:3). However, the book of Ecclesiastes 10:8, declared "He that diggeth a pit shall fall into it; and whoso breaketh a hedge, a serpent shall bite him." There is a hedge of protection around God's people, but if there's a hole in that hedge, it can open the door to the enemy and we can get bitten.

Paul warned the believers in Ephesians 4:27, "Neither give place to the devil." Also, 2 Corinthians 2:11 tells us, "Lest Satan should get an advantage of us: for we are not ignorant of his devices." Demons are expertise in transmitting diseases and illness as seen in the scriptures; Luke 13:10-16, Matt 17:15-18. Either the demon was there before the person came to Christ (past lifestyle, generational curse, bondages they previously came under, vows they made with the enemy, etc.), or it entered since they became a Christian. If the demon came into the person's life before they accepted Christ, then the demon is likely trespassing because he has no real legal right to be there, and simply needs to be cast out (as Jesus did in Matthew 8:16-17). The way demons gain access into a believer's life, is through open doors.

There are certain sins and things we can do that will defile us (make us unclean). For example, having unholy sex can create unholy soul ties, which serve as demonic bridges, and can pass bondages from one person to another. Another example is being bitter or unforgiving; both those are closely related and can defile a person (Hebrews 12:15). That evening after sunset the people brought to Jesus all the sick and demon-possessed. The whole town gathered at the door, and Jesus healed many who had various diseases. He also drove out many demons, but he would not let the demons speak because they knew who he was (Mark 1:32-34).

Jesus did two things in the above passage; He healed various diseases and drove out many demons. Demons are not interested in simply bringing physical infirmities, but they desire to ruin the spiritual life of the person, to destroy the eternal hope and to control your entire being. If anyone dies in this state of health, he/she goes to hell fire. The gift of discerning of spirits and the Holy Spirit will help us to certainly decide if an illness is of the devil. We should not give the devil a chance; we must avoid sin as it opens way for demonic attacks.

Mental Derangement and Torture

Satan can also inspire persecutors to make life hard for Christians even torture us to death. Like a church in Vietnam which the authorities demolished, arresting the pastor and beating ten others. You can read about a Muslim convert to Christianity in Iran, facing the death penalty for his conversion. You can read about a Christian woman in Eritrea whose six month old baby died two days after she was arrested under a charge of "actively witnessing about Christ". Even in some countries, it is legislated to punish any preach of the gospel. There are many such stories. It's harrowing stuff, and it is going on all over the world all the time: God's people suffering at the hands of evil men.

Paul knows that pain is the normal Christian experience, and the Apostle Peter agrees when he writes, Dear friends; do not be surprised at the painful trial you are suffering, as though something strange were happening to you for this pain is part of God's plan. God's purpose, as Paul puts it, is that we be conformed to the likeness of his Son. So, even in our suffering, God might be forming us into people who can comfort others in their suffering.

He might be calling us to a deeper relationship with Himself in prayer. He might be opening doors by our suffering into new worlds for us and His gospel. He is certainly teaching us to sort out what is important from what is unimportant in this world: to hold on less tightly to the things of this world, and to long more for the next. In all these ways God is making us more like Jesus, who himself suffered on our behalf. What He is doing in you to conform you to the likeness of His Son.

Furthermore, forgetfulness, frustration, confusion, doubt, skepticism, procrastination, indecision, self-delusion, unbelief, mind idolatry, resentment, temper, fear of rejection, insecurity, i nferiority,selfpity,anger,loneliness,prejuide,bitterness,unforgivenes s,jealousy,envy,daydreaming,hopelessness,despondency,insomnia, suicide,heaviness,burden,anxiety,nervousness,worry,fear,hallucina tions and depression are not sickness but mediums used by Satan to wreck and torture the mind of many.

For example, bitterness leads to diseases like cancer and arthritis; despair, discouragement and hopelessness open the door for colds and flu; rejection and self pity open the door for sinus infections. In the book of II Timothy 1:7 we were told that God did not give us a spirit of timidity (of cowardice, of craven and cringing and fawning fear), but of power and of love and of calm and well-balanced mind and discipline and self-control. We do not want to be driven by this fawning, craven, cringing fear. Therefore do not give devil a chance. In all the tricks and willies applied, he has a sole objective which is separating humanity from God, to raise evil throne in the mind and to manipulate on your desire to sin.

~ 8 ~

Demons and Sin

Can devil and his demons really make anyone of us (Christians) sin? No! He does tempt us at times, but it is we who choose whether or not to follow that temptation. Whatever desire is stronger in our heart is what prevails, for he cannot force us to sin. But many times it's easy to think of a "sinful nature" as something external that we can blame rather than admitting or taking the blame personally. We do not have anything inside us that causes us to sin, but rather it is we who sin.

It is the choice we made, if we should blame it on Satan, who shall Satan blame for sinning? If you do admit that it was your sinful nature that caused you to sin, make sure that you're not blaming something, but rather you choose to sin. We can also sin when we do what we are taught by men, we do not do what God's word says or set aside God's word and do what our parents have done (tradition). In addition, either from not seeing what we ought to do, or from not doing what we have already seen we ought to do; (of these two, the first is ignorance of the evil; the second, weakness) we sin. We always sin against God, but shall we continue in sin that grace may abound?

He that committeth sin is of the devil; for the devil sinneth from the beginning. For this purpose, the Son of God was manifested, that he might destroy the works of the devil. Whosoever is born of God doth not commit sin; for his seed remaineth in him: and he cannot sin, because he is born of God. In this the children of God are manifest, and the children of the devil; whosoever doeth not righteousness is not of God, neither he that loveth not his brother.

'Is of the devil' means that Satan has the legal right to do whatsoever he wants to a sinner. When we commit sin, we are directly calling Satan and his demons into our lives to influence and have dominion over our affairs. Sin fears no personality, the bishop that commits sin is of the devil, the pastor and members that commit sin is of the devil. He has his abode in them because it is not a thing of religious status. Sin is transgression of the law of God. It is anything contrary {thought, speech or action that brings darkness to our understanding and life} to God's perfect nature as well as his commandment. Sin defiles the mind and conscience Titus 1:15.

Some people can lie and never lose any sleep. They can steal, commit immoralities, and it never seems to upset them. Some can comfortably do evil and feel no remorse or disturbed for he has a defiled mind; an evil conscience. A sinful conscience calls evil good and good evil; that put darkness for light, and light for darkness; that put bitter for sweet, and sweet for bitter. It takes lightly the Word of God, especially that part that condemns sinful activity and thinks improperly about God and sin. A defiled mind is a step away from immoralities and sinful behaviors this is because unto the pure all things are pure: but unto them that are defiled and unbelieving is nothing pure; but even their mind and conscience is defiled. In Zechariah 3:3, sin was referred to as a "filthy garment. Sin as a filthy garment could best be described as a menstrual rag, filthy rags or grease-stained rags.

It is likened to a disgustingly offensive piece of cloth that is old, dirty or torn. No one would appear before His Majesty in a blood stained or dirty clothe. Everyone would like to appear in best fashion he or she could afford but most times, we appear before the Almighty God with a blood stained clothe. Sin corrupts and contaminates; it is the filthiness of the flesh and spirit, rebellious in nature, as Leviticus 26:27 says, walking "contrary" to God.

Sin has its roots in the heart, influences the intellect, and will, then find manifestations through the body. Prov.4:3; Mt.15:19-20; Lk.6:45; Heb.3:12; Jm1:14-15. The effects of sin are moral and spiritual bondages, guilt, death, and hell as James explained: Each person is tempted when he is lured and enticed by his own desire. Then desire when it has conceived gives birth to sin; and sin when it is full-grown brings forth death". The wages of all sin is spiritual and physical death. (Rom. 6:23; I Corinthians. 15:56). In 1st Kings 8:38, sin in man's heart was compared to ugly, oozing sores from a deadly plague. Like the stench of graves and rotten sepulchers, it pollutes a holy atmosphere. It enslaves the will of man. Rom.7:18-19.

Sin is ingratitude.

Everything we have, everything we are, is from God. It is by His infinite mercy that we live, move, and have our freedom Acts 17:28. God makes the sun to rise on the evil and the good, sends rain on the just and the unjust. He has given us everything we need; to crown it all sent His only begotten son to rescue us from a destined eternal doom. However, when we knew God, we did not glorify Him as God, neither were thankful.

God gave the food we eat, the air that we breathe. All the joys the sinner ever experienced, God provided. Every beauty of life is from God. He gave wisdom to every human being to think, feel, work, play and rest; that life might be full and useful. In addition, God made us love, made us laugh, and made us cry. And it's God who gave us special skills and abilities to excel in our endeavors, and to know some measure of self-respect and value. God gave us the capacity to care for each other and have relationships. Amidst of all He has done for us, we could not say thank you Lord. This is the worst ungratefulness.

Whenever we sin, there are consequences that follow, some of these consequences are spiritual and some are physical. As Adam and Eve had experienced both physical and spiritual consequences of their sin, so is everyone liable to this curse (Genesis 3).

1. Spiritual Death.

This is broken relationship between man and God, a state in which the human soul is separated from God and has not been enlivened by his Spirit, as seem in the scriptural verses below. Eph.4:18, Rom.8:6, Jam.1:15, Gen.2:17, John.5:24; 8:51, Luke.15:32. Adam and Eve did die a spiritual death immediately they ate the fruit. Their sin separated them from God (Isaiah 59:2), but in their spiritual death, they also began to die physically. A man without Christ is spiritually dead. Paul describes it as being alienated from the life of God, in Ephesians 4:18.

The book of Ephesians, chapter 2:1, gives us a safe and satisfactory answer. "And you hath He quickened (that is, made alive,) who were dead in trespasses and sins." This shows what sort of death is contemplated--a death in sin. The general scope of the Epistle shows that the apostle is conceiving of the state of lost sinners, fearfully depraved, as being dead; that is, he uses the term, death, by a figure of speech, to denote their terrible apathy on the subject of their guilt, danger, and fearful condition as exposed to the curse of God. A careful attention to the scope of this epistle will show this most fully. We may revert to Rom. 8:6, for a more specific description of this spiritual death. In this passage Paul says--"To be carnally-minded is death, but to be spiritually-minded is life and peace." The precise sense of the original is this; "the minding of the flesh is death;" the giving up of the mind to the demands of the flesh is utter ruin to the soul; because, says verse 7, "the minding of the flesh is enmity against God," and this enmity against God at once constitutes a state of spiritual death and must of course prove the eternal ruin of the soul. Reverting again to the train of thought and illustration pursued in Paul to the Ephesians, we read;--"You hath He quickened, who were dead in trespasses and sins; wherein in time passed ye walked according to the course of this world, according to the prince of the power of the air, the spirit that now worked in the children of disobedience: among whom also we all had our conversation in times past in the lusts of our flesh, fulfilling the desires of the flesh and of the mind; and were by nature the children of wrath, even as others.

But God, who is rich in mercy, for his great love wherewith He loved us, even when we were dead in sins, hath quickened us together with Christ: (by grace are ye saved:) and hath raised us up together, and made us sit together in heavenly places, in Christ Jesus," This death, therefore, as we see, is a death in sin--not one in which the mind is sunk into utter inactivity--not a state in which no action is possible; but simply one in which the mind acts, and the individual "walks according to the course of this world, according to the prince of the power of the air"--the same Satanic agency which energizes in all those who are disobedient to God. It is a death unto God, and to his character and claims.

The dead sinner is regardless of God and of God's rightful authority as one physically dead is of the natural world. The man physically dead is unconscious of what passes around him; he is borne to his grave, but he knows not by whom;--so the spiritually dead are voluntarily insensible to the great facts of the spiritual world--insensible to God, to truth, and to their own relations to both. They may be intensely alive to the things of the natural world, to everything relating to earthly pleasure; but to God and duty, they are dead. This sin brought death to the whole creation (Romans 8:18-23). The first type of spiritual death is the actual separation from God that automatically comes upon all born into mortality because of the fall of Adam.

The book of Revelation speaks of a second death, which is a final and eternal separation from God. Only those who have never experienced new life in Christ will partake of the second death. Revelation 2:11; 20:6, 14; 21:8). When we are born again, the spiritual death is reversed. Before salvation, we were spiritually dead, but Jesus gave us life. As it is written, you hath he quickened [made alive], who were dead in trespasses and sins; even when we were dead in sins, hath quickened us together with Christ. And you, being dead in your sins hath he quickened together with him, having forgiven you all trespasses. Colossians 2:13; Ephesians 2:1, 2:5. All mortals will be redeemed from this death, as well as from physical death, through Christ's Atonement and resurrection to be brought back into God's presence to stand before him. 1 Corinthians 15:21-23;

2. Physical consequences of sin.

Do not be deceived; God will not be mocked; whatever a man sow, that shall he also reap. Galatians 6:7. The punishment of sin is in two parts, each composed of two parallel clauses as it was on our progenitor. The first part deals with childbearing and the second with marital relations. With two quick strokes God illustrates the bane of women throughout the ages. The woman too received punishment for her sin. Just like the serpent, the punishment did not just affect her, but also all those who came after her. The first punishment was that childbirth would no longer be easy. It will be filled with sorrow and pain.

The second punishment was that the woman would no longer be emotionally independent. She would become emotionally bonded to her husband, becoming the follower, with the husband being the head of the family. Some women fight against this natural law, but it is a fact that this law exists. The man would have to labor hard for a living. The earth would no longer cooperate and make it easy to earn a living. Even to this day, it is the man's responsibility to earn a living for his family. The second half of the punishment is the affirmation of Adam, and all mankind's, eventual death. The last consequence of Adam and Eve was banishment from the Garden.

To this day, the physical consequence to sin varies with the sin committed. Some of these consequences are immediate while some comes later. As smokers are liable to die young so are fornicators liable to contact deadly diseases. A sinner might suffer all kinds of afflictions, disease and illness, minor or severe, slight or incurable in his body, ruined in his mind with all kinds of maladjustments, breakdowns and imbalances. There could be conflict, disorder and lack of harmony with others resulting to addictions, bondage, anguish, fear, shame, restlessness, anger, stress, sadness, depression, and life without meaning.

Sinner's social relationships with others manifests corruption, oppression, exploitation of the weak, injustice, violence, slavery, colonialism, imperialism, the search for power and dominion, racial conflicts and wars, segregation and marginalization, misery and hunger, manipulation of the mass media and factual information. The earth is seriously damaged: the air, springs, rivers, lakes, and oceans are contaminated. Forests are being razed. Animal species are becoming extinct and our natural resources are being abused and destroyed. Nature humiliates us for our sins. The physical consequence of sin knows no limit as it eventually invites the wrath of God. As sin alienates us from divine protection so does it give Satan and demons a stronghold to influence and control our lives.

However, there is remedy for all condemnation of sin for Christ put away sin through His sacrifice. Therefore, there is no condemnation to those who are in Christ Jesus (Romans 8:1). Christ displaced sin with His sacrifice; He took away its base. For this reason, Paul may say: Sin shall not have dominion over you (Romans 6:14). Sin, which was reigning in the world since Adam, was left without strength, without breath, without any power; sin was overcome by the sacrifice of Christ. Through His sacrifice, we have been set free from sin (Romans 6:22); we are not under the chains of sin; we are now acquitted from the condemnation to which we were subjected before.

Through faith in Him, we receive the fruits of His sacrifice, a sacrifice whose purpose was to save us and to free us from sin, for as in Adam all die, even so in Christ all shall be made alive (1 Corinthians 15:22). The gift and the grace of God were larger than the damage of sin. The most wonderful aspect of this plan to heal the sins of the world is that the gift and the grace are larger than the sin and transgression; Paul says: But the free gift is not like the offense. For if by the one man's offense (Adam's) many died, much more the grace of God and the gift by the grace of the one Man, Jesus Christ, abounded to many (Romans 5:15).

The redemptive work of Christ was so perfect that, it not only repaired the evil done by sin, but it set a new order, the grace, which is more perfect than the justice that Adam had before his sin. That is why Paul says: much more the grace of God and the gift abounded too many. Where sin abounded, grace abounded much more. These words of Paul refer to that sphere of grace where the believer is introduced by his faith in Jesus Christ. According to his words, grace went farther than sin, since where sin abounded, grace abounded much more (Romans 5:20).

This is the strongest way Paul was able to ponder the sphere of grace as opposed to sin. The reign of sin does not exist any more for believers; that is something from the past; there is only the reign of grace now, because as sin reigned in death, even so grace might reign through righteousness to eternal life through Jesus Christ our Lord (Romans 5:21). We are then dead to sin but alive to God, as the Apostle said: reckon yourselves to be dead indeed to sin, but alive to God in Christ Jesus our Lord (Romans 6:11).

~ 9 ~

THE STRONGHOLDS OF
DEMONIC INFLUENCES

Every pattern or attitude in our lives has a spiritual root-either good or bad. In the case of bad patterns or attitudes, unless the spiritual root is addressed, there can be no deliverance, although on the surface it may be possible to cover up before men. Jesus said "unless you first bind the strong man, you cannot plunder his goods" (Matt. 12:29). Demons cannot enter ones life anytime they like, they need a legal opening to gain entrance, so in order to get demons out, we usually need to know what it was that gave them the legal right to enter in the first place! Then by renunciation of that thing through a determined faith in God, we can, with God's authority, command the related demons to leave that we might live a life worthy of our calling.

When you repeatedly and intentionally violated your conscience or acted on a lie, your sense of right and wrong will be clouded, confused and darkened as the lie begins to take root. This will be formidable because believing a lie about a sinful act can create a stronghold in the mind. It can lead to other destructive patterns of thinking as the stronghold is interwoven not only with the brain but with our daily thoughts and memories. Over time, the victim will be manipulated and ultimately controlled by demonic impulses. The obvious indication of a possessed person occurs when there is no longer any concern for right and wrong; the person inflicts crimes of passion that are unimaginable.

Secondly, if you were sexually and/or emotionally abused during childhood, research revealed a strong possibility that you will grow up with thoughts and behaviors that are harmful and self destructive. These behaviors can range from self-loathing to bursts of hostility and hatred toward anyone who may innocently hurt your already hurting heart. Whether the anger is directed inwardly or outwardly, anger and frustration left unchecked can open a door for demonic possession. Thirdly, your mind is often the battlefield; for the devil can manipulate a strong influence over our minds using fantasies and hateful desires that demand a horrible and depraved fulfillment. Let us consider some of the basic strongholds of demonic influence in the lives of Christians.

TITHING

Inclusively, tithe avoidance is an insignificant doorway for demons in the life of many Christians. Many willfully avoid paying tithe while others because they lack proper teaching on the concept. You can tithe without loving God with all your heart, but you cannot love God with all your heart without tithing! My concern is on the willful, rebellious and disobedient Christians. Jesus clearly taught us to keep his commandments if we really love Him. It is required of us to observe and obey all the commandments of God without exception; guilty of one is guilty of all. There is no justification to any spirit of disobedience; sin is sin so matter how small or big. Tithing blesses, while tithe evasion is obviously a reproach. God only commanded us to pay 10 percent of our earning as a sign of obedience and gratefulness for his blessing. This is not optional rather a commandment. I wish to clearly remind and refurbish many Christians about the concept of tithing and jeopardizes of its disobedience.

Tithing is one of God's means of bringing us into maturity and prosperity. Tithing honors the Lord. Tithing demonstrates our faith in God's power to supply all our needs. We receive peace of mind knowing we are obeying God's Word. Tithing allows God to bless the remaining 90% of our income. Tithing blesses the church by enabling it to carry out a greater ministry to the world. Through our obedience to God in tithing, we become good examples of financial stewardship in God's Kingdom. If we are responsible to render our dues, tribute, custom, fear, and honor to earthly government, how much more so of our Lord Jesus Christ! In the simplest terms, if we are members of Christ's Kingdom, then we must pay its taxes - the tithe! Malachi 3 vs.8-12 is a very common passage to the ears of every Christian. Will a man rob God? Yet you rob me but you ask how we rob you, in tithes and offering. You are under a curse, the whole nation of you because you are robbing me"

I suggest we retrace the meaning of the following words: Rob means to steal. Taking what does not belong to you. In other words, stealing or I may call you a thief. Curse: an appeal for evil to befall someone or a consequence of sin. Devourers: Satan and his cohorts. The grammar is clear, pay and be blessed, refused and be cursed. Who shall rescue us from the curse of God, no one! It is sinful to take away things that belong to all merciful God. If tithe evasion is not sin, I still wonder why the book of Leviticus instructs us to add a fifth of the value to redeem our tithe. Leviticus 27:30-31.

Tithe evasion defiles us, denies us of God's blessings and opens us up to Devil for torture. When we deny and deprive God of this share of our earnings, Satan and his demons automatically gains a legal ground into our business, into our children even our lives. However, If we can Budget our earnings, Acknowledge the Lordship of Jesus over material possessions; Become conscious that our prosperity and productivity is a gift of God; Believe the church is primarily instituted by God to promote worship, teaching; Care for evangelism and mission work; Understand that the success of a church depends on faithful tithers;

Understand that the blessings of God are directly in proportion to faithfulness and obedience; Believe that tithing is the key to financial freedom and liberation from financial incapacitations; Understand the importance of honoring our spiritual leaders by providing adequate life support, so that they could pay proper attention in their calling; (I Timothy 5:17,18), Wish to come to God in prayer without embarrassment; Learn that the only way to be free from grid of materialism is to give cheerfully; Be convinced that God's gifts are much greater than ours (Luke 6:38); Simply believe the Bible is God's Word, and is still binding today, then we should see reasons to pay our tithe. Tithe belongs to God and its evasion is very disastrous.

ANCESTRAL / GENERATIONAL SIN

Literally, this means the sins our progenitors committed. To what extent does their sin have effect on us? Can we be exonerated from the consequence of their sin? As the book of Deuteronomy 5:9,10 declared For I , the Lord your God, am a jealous God, visiting the iniquity of the fathers upon the children to the third and fourth generations of those who hate Me, but showing mercy to thousands, to those who love Me and keep my commandment. Also in Exodus 20:3-5 God further declared that the children will be punished for the sin of their fathers.

In fact, God says up to the fourth generation may experience this punishment. Does this mean that a child must bear the punishment for a sin he or she did not commit? Would not God be unjust or at best contradictory when the Bible says that each person will only be held guilty for their individual sin? (Deut. 24:16, Ezek. 18:20) though each person is held accountable before God for his/her own sins.

Each person, however, may suffer the consequences of anyone's sin. A robber who sprays a bank hall with machine guns may wound or kill many innocent victims. They certainly are being "punished" for the sins of the robber. But they are not punished in the sense of being culpable for the crime. Rather, they suffer the consequences of his lawless behavior.

Each of us has two parents, four grandparents, eight great-grand parents and sixteen great-great grand parents, summarily a sum of 36 persons are involved in our life. It is very possible that one of them might cause a demon to act in our life either by oath, occultic participation, sin or even sacrifice. This determines and strongly reminds every Christian on how serious we should pray for our lives because if there had been a curse laid, sin committed, idolatry, murder or whatever sin committed by one among the 36 persons, it would be a hidden source of trouble in our lives as sins of David were repeated in the lives of both Absalom and Solomon.

Sometimes this influence begins right from the womb even to an untimely death. The consequences of idolatry and occult sins are transmitted to the third and fourth generations of those who hate God and demons have this as legal ground to influence even the unborn babies of such generation. Though most Christians reject this concept of ancestral curses with the belief Jesus took them all away, I do not object forasmuch we do not confess Christ with our lips while our lives partially denies Him.

Evidently, Medical science has proven the existence of generational medical issues such as diabetes, sickle cell anemia and even drug/alcohol addiction, hence to question this generational concept is not intellectually wise. In the book of Matthew 5:17, Jesus stated, "Do not think that I am come to destroy the Law or the Prophets. I did not come to destroy but to fulfill." Therefore, the concept of Generational sin is valid as far as the New Testament bible is concern. This is reason why Apostle Paul advised us to work out our salvation with fear and trembling.

After accepting Christ in our life, the work we do towards salvation is called sanctification. So, sanctification is the part of the salvation process that covers those iniquities that were bequeathed to us from former generations. If we are truly born again Christians, what about our children, are they born again?

I was born in a Christian family, my parents are true Christians committed members of Assemblies of God church but I gave my life to Christ at my age of 20. What happened to my past 19 years? Truly I say unto unless we all have totally submitted to Christ, we are bound by these curses even our children.

The Mirror of Ancestral Sins

There was a time in King David regime when a severe drought devastated the nation. Most of us would have dismissed it as a mere random natural occurrence. We would have simply endured it, while praying for rain and the drought would have continued. David, however, had a deeper understanding of the supernatural. He earnestly sought the Lord as to the reason for the drought. God response was astounding. He revealed that the drought was due to suffering inflicted on a pagan tribe by Saul, the previous king. By his action, Saul was not breaking a covenant that he himself had made with these people. It was just a covenant made many generations before him, right back in Joshua time.

None of this was David doing. Saul was already dead and was not even an ancestor of David. In fact, Saul and David were enemies. Nevertheless, David and all his generation were suffering because of Saul actions. Amazingly, this drought was not the continuation of one that had commenced during Saul reign. It did not even begin until well into David reign. Yet it all had its source in the actions of the previous generation in breaking a covenant made by a still earlier generation. What happens in earlier generations is clearly of great spiritual importance.

As it is the norm for generational curses, no one salvation was at stake, but physical and material hardship occurred until the source was identified and specific action was taken to remedy it. Like a fluttering sparrow or a darting swallow, an undeserved curse does not come to rest (Proverbs 26:2), but even though

David himself was innocent and enjoyed full forgiveness for his personal sins, this curse continued because it was deserved.

The Bible reveals that there was an offense someone other than David had committed that David needed to acknowledge and deal with. David asked the offended pagans what he should do in order for them to bless the Israelites. David asked the Gibeonites, what shall I do for you? How shall I make amends so that you will bless the Lord's inheritance (2 Samuel 21:3).

It seems from this that they had been cursing Israel, and David wanted them to reverse the curse. The Lord had allowed this curse to affect His people because the pagans' grievance was legitimate. It was not enough for David to pray for rain. Nor was it enough for him to ask God forgiveness for Saul's actions. David had to put right the injustice done to these people before God answered his prayer for rain (2 Samuel 21:1-14)."...Grantley Morris.

Lest we dismiss this as Old Testament as though God's fundamental character could change, **Jesus himself taught this truth** in Luke 11:50-51, He declared, therefore this generation will be held responsible for the blood of all the prophets that has been shed since the beginning of the world, from the blood of Abel to the blood of Zechariah, who was killed between the altar and the sanctuary. Yes, I tell you, this generation will be held responsible for it all.

However, the reason many Christians do not bother to activate God's deliverance from curses is that they confuse the curse of the law with other curses. This confusion leads people to wrongly presume that just because they are protected from the curse of breaking the Mosaic Law, they are automatically protected from quite different curses without needing to pray or specifically believe for those curses to be broken in their lives.

The effects of the sins or curse on our progenitors might be active in our lives because they brought us to earth. This is quite different from the curse by our personal sins. Nehemiah said, they stood in their places and confessed their sins and the wickedness of their fathers. Jeremiah cried, we have sinned against the Lord our God, both we and our fathers. Therefore, we must confess and break these generational curses through the Power in the name of Jesus.

PERSONAL SIN

Personal Sin is anything we think, say, or act upon which goes against the Holy character of God; that means the proclivity to act contrary to the Holy nature of God, plan, purpose, and will. It hinders believer's fellowship with God and gives the devil a foothold in the believer's life. Although sins are forgiven completely at the moment of salvation, the believer still struggles to live in the Spirit as opposed to the flesh (Rom. 7:21-25). If this sin is confessed (1 John 1:7, 9), the believer is restored in fellowship with God. If the believer fails to confess this sin (1 John 1:8), by his actions he makes God a liar for God has already condemned sin as worthy of death (Gen. 2:17, Mark 9:47, Rom. 8:3).

One cannot be filled (continually controlled) with the Holy Spirit, as we are commanded in Eph. 5:18, and at the same time harbor un-confessed sin in his life. However, both unbelievers and Christians commit sin every day ranging from seemingly innocent fibs to murder, this made a believer vulnerable to all kinds of fleshly enticements and worldly lusts. {For a just mall shall fall seven times and shall rise again: but the wicked shall fall down into evil}. Satan can also use guilt and shame a believer feels to push him farther away from God, away from prayer, Bible study, Christian fellowship, and any other avenue whereby he might confront God concerning his sin.

This is a prize which the devil will relish and never release until the believer exercises the repentance and confession necessary to restore his fellowship. In this context, I want to illustrate more on sexual sins as a stronghold for demonic invasion. These include fornication, adultery, incest, bestiality, homosexuality {lesbianism/gay}, masturbation and harlotry.

FORNICATION/SEX ADDICTION.

Defining fornication as sexual relationship between singles gives it no full meaning because incest and bestiality are forms of it that can occur between married and singles. Fornication is the sexual relationship between two or more people whether married or singles. Sexual intercourse is supposed to be for the married ones alone; violation of this rule creates an unholy spiritual bondage between you and can as well cause demonic subjugations in your life.

Uncontrollable desire for sexual satisfaction is referred to as sexual addiction. It is without a doubt one of the most common and soul-destroying forms of addictions in existence. "Without purity of heart, we cannot fully enjoy God". Fornication brings down your progress, ruins your business and most dangerously keeps you very far from God.

It dehumanizes, animalizes and brutalizes you both physically and spiritually. Those involved therein grows continually more coarse, less sensitive, having less regard for the welfare of others, self centered, more desirous of having only their own needs met.

Fornication is the proximate cause of immoralities because it usually set in motion a train of sinful events in the life of a sexual addict; murder and abortion. The book of 2 Samuel chapter 11 clearly illustrate how King David's loneliness gave birth to fornication, fornication gave birth to murder which led to "covetousness and fulfillment of self desire". Consequently, David was cursed by God through Nathan the Prophet; "the sword will never leave your family". Apostle Paul knew that once a Christian is neutralized, disconnected, and dismantled of his divine coverage, he automatically become vulnerable to any plague of Satan.

Therefore he cautioned us in the book of Ephesians 5 verses 3 but among you there must not be even a hint of sexual immorality, or of any kind of impurity, or of greed, because these are improper for God's holy people. 1 Corinthians 10 verses 8…We should not commit sexual immorality, as some of them did--and in one day twenty-three thousand of them died. Sex addiction leads to compulsive masturbation, extra marital affairs, multiple sexual partners, consistent use of pornography, unsafe sex, phone sex, prostitution, exhibitionism, obsessive dating, voyeurism, sexual harassment and even rape.

Voyeurism is a disorder that involves achieving sexual arousal by observing an unsuspecting and non-consenting person who is undressing, unclothed, naked bodies or sexual acts of others, especially from a secret vantage point. The voyeur does not seek sexual contact with the person he is observing. Another name for this behavior is "peeping". Legal consequences of sexual addiction result when illegal behaviors such as voyeurism, exhibitionism, or inappropriate touching, result in arrest and incarceration.

Adultery

This is an illicit sexual intercourse outside marriage or sexual relations between a married person and someone not the spouse. There is nothing more consecrated in God's sight than marriage. It is God's institution and plan for His creatures. The first institution that God made was the home. He said in Genesis 2:18 that it is not good for man to live alone, so He made a woman, an help meet for him; and told the first couple—the first family, the first man and wife, Adam and Eve—to be fruitful and multiply and to replenish the earth.

Dear friend, this is the reason why homosexuality and lesbianism is such an abomination in the sight of God, because man to woman is the only God-appointed means to multiply the earth, thus our matrimonial bed should not be defiled.

The evil consequences of adultery are too strong and begin to manifest immediately. When the family is shattered by adultery, every member of that family suffers. When a man takes his neighbor's wife, he breaks up two homes; he takes another man's property and deprives him of his rights and his own wife's rights which God has given them. When a woman takes another woman's husband, she deprives her of her rights and the rights of her husband.

Then the children are deprived of their rights to the love of both parents and the authority of love which should characterize home as God's institution of discipline and instruction. Not only this, but the heartache, sorrow, suffering, tears and privation that stay for a lifetime unless sweetened by the cross of Christ. I am very sure that untold millions are experiencing this major consequence of adultery in our society today. This is certainly Satan's master stroke against our nation today, to so undermine the home, all the fabric of our society will become loose and our nation will fall into utter ruin.

More so, as couples become one flesh upon their marriage which is consummated by sexual intercourse thus oneness of the marital union is holy by nature, so it is when we commit sexual sin with someone other than our mate, an unholy bond is established. Several scriptural passages out-rightly condemned adultery as punishable by "death'. See Exodus 20:14; Deut 22:22; Leviticus 20:10; Proverbs 6:32.

Incest

This is another branch of fornication that brings serious links and doorways for demons into a generational descent. It is the sexual relations between close relatives where their marriage is illegal or forbidden by custom. Though you may ask me this question 'If God created Adam and Eve doesn't that mean that their offspring would have to eventually commit incestuous sexual intercourse in order to populate the land?

Rightly put, Cain married his blood sister. This in no doubt is very correct. Genesis 5:4 tells us that Adam and Eve "begat sons and daughters." Therefore, brothers must have married sisters at the beginning. Remember that the law against close intermarriage was not given until the time of Moses—e.g. "none of you shall approach to any that is near of kin to him" Leviticus 18:6.

Originally, there was nothing wrong with brother and sister marriages. If you think about it, that is the only way to populate the world, starting with only one pair. Notice that Abraham married his half sister with no condemnation from God, even though this was later forbidden. Adam and Eve were created perfect; their genes would have been perfect. But as the curse God placed on humanity became effective, their descendants would have had many mistakes in their genes. So brothers and sisters (Adam and Eve's children) could have married and not had the problems of deformities in their offspring as might well happen today, if such close relatives married and had children. This is because today humans have lots of mistakes—because of the curse—in their genes.

This may cause problems when matching pairs are inherited from both parents, as is much more likely with close intermarriage. Thus came about the commandment against incest. If a man has relations with his daughter that is incest and fornication. If a mother had relations with her son this is incest and fornication. (1 Corinthians 5:1) If a brother and sister (married or not) have relations it is incest.

Incest is fornication; married or not. God and humanity seriously forbid this act. The following scriptural verses condemned incest; "No one is to approach any close relative to have sexual relations. I am the Lord...Everyone who does any of these detestable things -- such persons must be cut off from their people" (Leviticus 18:6, 29). If a man sleeps with his father's wife... his daughter-in-law...a woman and her daughter...his sister, the daughter of either his father or his mother...it is a disgrace. They must be cut off before the eyes of their people...he will be held responsible" (Leviticus 20:11, 12, 14, 17).

For John had said unto Herod, it is not lawful for you to have your brother's wife" (Mark 6:18).

It is actually reported that there is sexual immorality among you, and of a kind that does not occur even among pagans: A man has his father's wife...hand this man over to Satan, so that the sinful nature may be destroyed and his spirit saved on the day of the Lord" (I Corinthians 5:1, 5). Rather, clothe yourselves with the Lord Jesus Christ, and do not think about how to gratify the desires of the sinful nature" (Romans 13:14).

Bestiality

This is a sexual relationship with animals. It is commonly seen among Asian and European ladies where pets especially dogs, cats and horses are specially trained as sex mates. Bestiality degrades the image of God in man. Man is not an animal, but the crown of creation. It is dirty indeed, even from a customary point of view demonized, defiling, demoralized and untraditional.

The Bible condemned this act- 'If a man has sexual relations with an animal, he must be put to death, and you must kill the animal. If a woman approaches an animal to have sexual relations with it, kill both the woman and the animal. They must be put to death, their blood will be on their own heads". Leviticus 20:15-16."Anyone who has sexual relations with an animal must be put to death' Exodus 22:19."Do not have sexual relations with an animal and defile yourself with it. A woman must not present herself to an animal to have sexual relations with it; that is a perversion' Leviticus 18:23. This sexual activity incurs full penalty under God's law and Satan uses this medium to possess the life of the participants.

Cross-dressing and Transvestism

Cross-dressing is the act of wearing clothes commonly associated with opposite gender within a particular society while transvestism is the practice of cross-dressing, which is wearing the clothes of the opposite sex. It is a form of behavior in which a person has a compulsive desire to dress in the clothes of the opposite sex. In this situation, the person adopts the dress and often the behavior typical of the opposite sex for the purpose of emotional and sexual gratification. Transvestite refers to a person who cross-dresses; however, the word often has additional connotations.

Clothing was instituted by God (Gen. 3:21) to hinder and prevent sin not to encourage it. Any clothing that accent, emphasizes, or exposes the intimate parts of our bodies- buttocks, breasts, crotch, or a delicately formed thigh is not only immodest but sexually provocative to the lusts of sinful men. (Isaiah. 20:4; 47:3) Personally, I cannot see how Christians can militantly oppose homosexuality and its deviate life-style without opposing and exposing its deviate dress style Transvestism is clearly an evil appearance. We are warned to abstain from all appearance of evil.1 Thessalonica 5:22. It is disobedience to God for a woman to wear anything that pertains to a man or for a man to put on a woman's garment; it is an abomination before the Lord your God. Deuteronomy 22:5. It is immodesty because women adorn themselves in modest apparel.--1Timothy 2:9.

Though some of the Deuteronomic code is not followed these days, because many of the laws are ridiculous by current moral standards but God's standard does not change with time and season. Other related terminologies in this concept are:

Drag queen: this is usually referred to a man who dresses in female clothes and make-up for special occasions and entertainment.

Drag kings are mostly female performance artists who dress in masculine clothes and personify male gender stereotypes as part of their performance.

Transsexual or Transgender

This is an act of having a psychological urge to belong to the opposite sex that may be carried out to the point of undergoing medical surgery to modify the sex organs just to mimic the opposite sex. Transsexuals desire to have different physical gender from that which they were assigned at birth, so they undergo series of surgical treatment to change their anatomical sex. Transsexual transition is a life journey that requires time, money, decision about your destination and it is irreversible.

The extreme hormonal manipulation and surgical mutilations involved in transsexual operations are not justifiable unless the health of the homosexual were at stake. Trans-sexuality is living a lie, a foolish fantasy. Neither Biblical exegesis nor research science gives credibility to the transsexual's insistence that he or she is the opposite sex caught in an opposite sex body. The transsexual thoughts, desires, feelings amount to nothing more than an elaborate, expensive, moral-mental delusion.

That a lie can be so addictive should not surprise the Christian ethicist as the book of Romans 1 and 6:12-18 have clearly illustrated the addictive nature and power of sin. Ephesians 4:17-19, 22 teaches us that the deceitful desires which lead to a greedy lust for more impurity have a progressive quality. Not to call this sin "sin", especially when it is within yourself, is to be caught in the web of self-deception. Medical science has helped raise this delusion to new heights. Now surgery renders a body outwardly closer to this moral-mental delusion. Yet, the genetic witness remains!

If transvestism is abhorrent to God, then a radical surgical "dressing up" is far worse. If the lesser sin of transvestism is an abomination, then transsexual operations must be super abomination. This is a clear truth that almost all transvestites have a female name to go with the female wardrobe. Nowhere is the difference between the sex assigned by nature and the gender identity acquired through social conditioning more dramatically demonstrated than in the transsexual. The man knows he is a male and yet rejects his manliness. Typically a man will undergo transsexual surgery because he wants to be perceived as and/or loved as a woman by a "straight" man. He does not wish to be loved by a homosexual whose love-sex object is another man.

The transsexual is firmly convinced that some cruel caprice of nature has imposed upon him; the body of a male, emotionality and mentality of a woman. Satan blinds and binds transsexuals through such lies. Few transsexuals ever go back to their God-given gender. The pastoral counselor or physician cannot in good conscience encourage such bondage. The universal response to transsexual operations must be "no", "never". The Bible views any deliberate damage to the body as an insult of great magnitude. Paul teaches that the body is the temple of the Holy Spirit and should be protected. 1 Corinthians 6:12-20.

The only God-given place to exercise companionship, complimentary gender identity, and bodily sexual gratification is within the bonds of marriage, 1 Corinthians 7:2, 9. Transgender opens the door to guilt and shame before God, Genesis. 3:8-10, 21, and before one's spouse, Genesis 2:25; 3:7. In cursing man, God said there would be abuse and conflict in the male-female, husband-wife relationship, Genesis 3:16. So, what could be the intention of clay telling the porter the style to mould? Why should women decide to stand up while urinating and why should men debased to squatting. This action does not reveal the glory of God. It desecrates a body made in the image of God. The thought of it and lust thereof is of the devil. However, I have good news for anyone involved therein, Whatever was your past, whatever you are now, male or female, what matters is you are in Christ as you have agreed to be buried with Him, you will rise with Him in newness of life, for if anyone is in Christ, he is a new creation; old things have passed away; behold, all things have become new.

Pedophilia

This is another branch of fornication that involves sexual preference of an adult for prepubescent; children. It gives demons a legal ground in the life of the sinner. A person with this attraction is called a pedophile or paedophile. Pedophiles are people who fall under the characteristic of one "without natural affection." (Romans 1:31; 2 Timothy 3:2). The phrase "without natural affection" is translated from one Greek word which means inhuman, unloving and unsociable or one who acts in ways that are against the social norm. It is a sexual relation/fantasy with a child. A sexual desire felt by an adult for children, or the crime of sex with a child. This does not portray holiness; it is a crime against humanity and a sin before God.

Homosexuality

Do you not know that the wicked will not inherit the kingdom of God? Do not be deceived: neither the sexually immoral nor idolaters nor adulterers nor male prostitutes nor homosexual offenders... will inherit the kingdom of God. 1 Corinthians 6:9 Homosexuality is having a preference for sexual relationship with or to feel attracted to person of the same sex.

It is a deep urge to sexual relationship with people of the same sex. Male homosexuals are referred to as gay {sodomites}; whereas female homosexuals are termed lesbians. The first reference to homosexuality in the Bible is found in Genesis 19 where Lot entertains two angels who come to the city to investigate its sins. Before they went to bed, all the men (from every part of the city of Sodom) surrounded the house and order him to bring out the men so that "we may know them.

''Know" in the above citation means to have sexual intercourse. Indeed, it will soon be unlawful in this country to classify homosexuals as sinners. Refined for our time, alternative lifestyle is now the favorite description of the way homosexuals choose to live. We are in the peak of the end time and many uncultured, unbiblical and irreligious doctrines have been emanated. The world is gradually in unity turning against the Word, trying to dilute it to their taste and style.

Fortunately, God did not leave without a word of advice. There is one basic truth and warning false prophets shall rise, that some group of people shares the same idea or create their own sect of acceptance about homosexual behavior does not make it right. They are only trying to falsify the teachings of Christ and must not be left unopposed. They make a mockery of Christianity. They are what the Apostle Paul describes as false apostles; the unorthodoxy doctrine. No matter any misleading idea from anyone, homosexuality is a sin.

Their condemnation is clear, two passages in Leviticus call homosexuality an abomination. Leviticus 18:22 says, "Do not lie with a man as one lies with a women; that is detestable."

Leviticus 20:13 says, "If a man lies with a man as one lies with a woman, both of them have done what is detestable." The word for "abomination" is used five times in Leviticus 18 and is a strong term of disapproval, implying that something is abhorrent to God. Because of this, God gave them over to shameful lusts. Even their women exchanged natural relations for unnatural ones. In the same way the men also abandoned natural relations with women and were inflamed with lust for one another. Men committed indecent acts with other men, and received in themselves the due penalty for their perversion. Romans 1:26-27. God created man and woman for the institution of marriage (Gen. 2:24). Homosexuality is a violation of the creation order, and God clearly condemns it as unnatural and specifically it is against His ordained order.

OCCULT PARTICIPATION

Any conscious or unconscious involvement in the occult is a personal request to be pestered by Satan. Evidence of the remarkable deceptive power of Satan is seen in the attitude shown by so many professing Christians regarding the label of "occultic" on such things as Ouija boards, astrology, and fortune-telling.

These are seen as trifles or childish games but in actual sense these activities are condemned by God in Deuteronomy 18; let no one be found among you who sacrifices his son or daughter in the fire, who practices divination or sorcery, interprets omens, engages in witchcraft, or casts spells, or who is a medium or spiritist or who consults the dead.

Anyone who does these things is detestable to the Lord, and because of these detestable practices the Lord your God will drive out those nations before you. (Deut. 18:10-12) The inhabitants of Canaan lost their homes, their land, and their lives because of these practices. Like personal sin, the believer's involvement in the occult takes things one step further. The believer opens himself up to more than just a beachhead for Satan.

Dabbling in occult practices leads the believer to become greatly deceived. Satan enjoys nothing more than a believer who starts trusting in mysticism, newly found powers, prophetic knowledge or anything to lead one away from trusting in God. When believer opens the door to spiritual oppression in a realm he knows little about, he will be unable to discern spiritual truth except for divine intervention.

THE TONGUE

What happens whenever we confess negative words? Who fulfills the curses and spells that we lay on others? Have you ever witness the devastating effects of gossips in the church? Please get this right, all the blessings that a Christian enjoy are just the spoken words of God {Tongue of God}. Whatever you say about yourself or about others may become a curse or blessing because the tongue has a great power in making and destroying dreams. God formed heaven and earth with His tongue, thus the tongue has a pre-ordained ability to create situation. Our words can motivate faith or instigate fear, as James said the tongue is a fire, a world of iniquity: so is the tongue among our members, that it defiles the whole body, and set on fire the course of nature; and it is set on fire of hell. Our tongues can bring misfortune and blessing not just to us alone but to the lives of people around us. Your kind words can help people while your negative words hurt - sometimes for a very long time. Positive, uplifting, encouraging words will lead to joy, peace and positive results while negative, depressing, hopeless words tears down, leads to depression and defeat.

Therefore, you can use words to speak life, health and blessing to yourself and to others. The Bible tells us in James 3:8-9, that the tongues can no man tame; it is an unruly evil, full of deadly poison. Therewith bless us God, even the Father; and therewith curse we men, which are made after the similitude (image) of God." Though Bible says that nobody can tame the tongue but, with the help of the Holy Spirit, you and I can be saved from the destructive power of our own words.

We can purposely order our conversation and speak carefully chosen words of God that will not only produce victory in our own life but in the lives of others as well. It is our privilege and responsibility as Christians to speak forth positive life-giving words in a world immersed in negativity. You are the Prophet of your own life; the words you spoke yesterday determined where you are today believe it or not. You created your today. Just as you will notice that everything surrounding Jesus' entire life (His birth, ministry, death, burial, and resurrection) was a direct fulfillment of what God's prophets had spoken.

Therefore, we must guard the words we speak. The Bible tells us in Colossians 4:6 *to let our speech be always with grace, seasoned with salt, that ye may know how ye ought to answer every man.* Ephesians 4:29-30 further says: Let no corrupt communication proceed out of your mouth, but that which is good to the use of edifying, that it may minister grace unto the hearers. And grieve not the Holy Spirit of God, whereby ye are sealed unto the day of redemption. Let all bitterness, and wrath, and anger, and clamor, and evil speaking, be put away from you, with all malice. We should also avoid jesting. The book of Ephesians 5:4 prohibits jesting (joking), foolish and silly talking.

Jokes are comment that can be easily turned to mean something else, to adapt to moods and conditions of those it is dealing with at the time. It is a polished and witty speech; an instrument of sin; refined versatility without Christian flavor or grace, lodged in a sly question; a smart answer; a hint; an insinuation; sarcasm; exaggeration; figurative expression; acute nonsense; unaccountable and inexplicable but in actual sense, it is a fancy windings of language convenient at the moment regardless of being exactly true. Jesus tells us in Matthew 5:26 to *let our yea be yea and your nay be nay, whatever is more than this comes from evil.*

In Mark 4:24, He further instructed us to be careful of what we hear also, because, what you hear will be multiplied unto you. Hear the words of life and receive life multiplied; hear the world and you have zero. So as we consider words, they have power when you speak them and they have power when you hear them. Satan and his demons seizes our negatively confessed words as a ground for their evil tidings

Death and life are in the power of the tongue says Solomon Proverb 18:21. A man's belly shall be satisfied with the fruit of his mouth and the increase of his lips shall he be filled Solomon added in verse 20. Whoso keepeth his mouth and his tongue keepeth his soul from troubles Proverb 21:23 having known the meaning of curse and its effects, every Christian should be extremely careful about the use of words. Our life could be curse as well as our children and entire generations from the words we profess. "As he loved cursing, so let it come unto him: as he delighted not in blessing, so let it be far from him. As he clothed himself with cursing like as with his garments, so let it come into his bowels like water and like oil in his bones" Psalms 109:17-18.

We should not curse rather bless and pray for our enemies because the soul of every man is important to God. Let us consider different kinds of tongues.

The lying tongue:"a man that beareth false witness against his neighbor is a maul and a sword and a sharp arrow"John8:44. Proverb 12:22 Lying lips are an abomination to Yahweh.

The swift tongue: Most Christians speak before thinking, forgetting that any word release cannot not be withdrawn."He that answereth a matter before he heareth it, it is folly and shame unto him" Proverbs 18:17.

The Backbiting tongue as warned in the books of Proverb 25:23 and Romans 1:30 sow a seed of discord among brethren.

Many churches are in dispute, families have scattered and lives ruined because of a word from just one tongue.

The tongue gossip is the tongue that murmurs and God hates murmuring, therefore shun profane and vain babblings: for they will increase to more ungodliness.

Some tongues flatters. Flattery is a sin of the tongue. The book of Psalms said "for there is no faithfulness in their mouth, their inward part is very wicked, their throat is an open sepulcher, and they flatter with their tongues.5:9.

The proud tongue "The Lord shall cut off all flattering lips and the tongue that speaketh proud things. Proverbs 18:13. A proud tongued Christian will talk much of his knowledge and service but very little about the Lord .Therefore the spirit in Satan that made him rebel against God dwells in him. God hates and despises the proud.

The overused tongue" a fool's voice is known by multitude of words" Ecclesiastes 5:3.

The Covetous Tongue: 2 Peter 2:3 and through covetousness shall they with feigned words make merchandise of you: whose judgment now of a long time lingereth not, and their damnation slumbereth not. 2 Peter 2:18 for when they speak great swelling words of vanity, they allure through the lusts of the flesh, through much wantonness, those that were clean escaped from them who live in error. The Bible vividly tells us about how powerful our words really are and how they can be used to bring life, either love, edification and encouragement into a person's life or bring death, destruction, and torment. The evil one usually uses our negatively confessed words to accomplish death, destruction and torment.

"Death and life are in the power of the tongue, and those who love it will eat its fruit."(Proverbs 18:21) "There is one who speaks like the piercing of a sword, but the tongue of the wise promotes health. The truthful lip shall be established forever, but a lying tongue is but for a moment." (Proverbs 12:18). "Keep your tongue from evil, and your lips from speaking guile. Depart from evil, and do good; seek peace, and pursue it." (Psalm 34:13). "A man's stomach shall be satisfied from the fruit of his mouth, and from the produce of his lips he shall be filled." (Proverbs 18:20)

"The Lord God has given me the tongue of the learned, that I should know how to speak a word in season to him who is weary." (Isaiah 50:4). "Walk in wisdom toward those who are outside, redeeming the time. Let your speech always be with grace, seasoned with salt, that you may know how you ought to answer each one." (Colossians 4:5)

"The mouth of the righteous is a well of life, but violence covers the mouth of the wicked." (Pro 10:11). "The words of a man's mouth are deep waters; the wellspring of wisdom is a flowing brook." (Pro 18:4). "A wholesome tongue is a tree of life, but perverseness in it breaks the spirit." (Proverbs 15:4). "Pleasant words are like a honeycomb, sweetness to the soul and health to the bones." (Proverbs 16:24)

"Anxiety in the heart of man causes depression, but a good word makes it glad." (Proverbs 12:25). "A soft answer turns away wrath, but a harsh word stirs up anger. The tongue of the wise uses knowledge rightly, but the mouth of fools pours forth foolishness." (Proverbs 15:1). "He who guards his mouth preserves his life, but he who opens wide his lips shall have destruction." (Proverbs 13:3)

"Whoever guards his mouth and tongue keeps his soul from troubles." (Proverbs 21:23)

"The heart of the righteous studies how to answer, but the mouth of the wicked pours forth evil." (Proverbs 15:28). "Set a guard, O Lord, over my mouth; keep watch over the door of my lips." (Psalm 141:3). Therefore, speak life and you will have it in abundance but speak death you will see destruction and failure at your doorstep.

UNHOLY HOMES:

"Neither shall thou bring an abomination into thine house, lest thou be a cursed thing like but thou shall utterly detest it, and thou shalt utterly abhor it; for it is a cursed thing." Deuteronomy 7:26

There will be terrible experiences or encounters whenever a Christian lives together with an occult member. As darkness and light are incompatible so shall this social habitation be, for evil encounters must arise ranging from nightmares to physical confrontations. But in many Christian homes, Satan has subtly crept in with simulative idea of making abominable things look "innocent". It may appear like a gift, souvenir, fashion and jewelries that literally have no spiritual connotation, in real sense; it could be his communicative gadgets.

The Word of God strongly advised us to put away the "strange gods" because demons are definitely attracted to homes where there are objects and literature that pertains to false religions, cults, the occult and spiritism. In our time, some of the accursed objects are: Buddha statutes, dolls and stuffed animals originated in voodoo, some fetish religious items passed down from ancestors, any kind of good luck charm, statues of other gods, oriental objects, most ancient African items, Indian items, American Indian items, any items that are used in witchcraft, divination, occult symbols, talisman, amulets, crystals used for guidance or healing, book of Mormon, satanic bible, books on other religions, rock and roll music, etc can be links for demons to your home.

CURSES, SPELLS, INCANTATION AND HEXES

These four accomplishes the same purpose. It is all about summoning a demon or demons through a spoken word {enchantment} to perform a given action in the life or affairs of others. The term placing a spell, hex or curse on someone could also be referred to as calling up a particular demon and sending it to a particular person to perform certain influences or damage.

All spells are accomplished by demons even the so-called "good ones" such as those stimulating love and riches in one's life.

Though these evil words could be repercussional or consequential for evil committed, demons are solely responsible for accomplishing this evil task. Also reading an occultic arts, playing with an Ouija board, trying to ESP, psychic experience, astral projection, any kind of meditation that involves clearing of the mind from thoughts, participation in magic of any kind, using the art of levitation, consulting a spiritist in an attempt to locate some missing object {many Christians often do this}, practice of any witchcraft, use of or abuse of street drugs, smuggling of any kind, repeated drunkenness, child abuse and the likes opens door to demons in our lives.

Many Christians are taking God's word for guaranteed, the consciousness of the impediments of sin no longer worry us, it is obvious that we are paying deaf ears to divine commandment as if we have bribed God but do not be deceive, the blessings of God equals His curses. Whenever we err or deviate from our spiritual standard, the consequences thereof could be seen as curse because sin opens us up to the world of misfortune and tragedies. The Bible expressly imposes curses when people sin, add or take away from the Word of God.

Deuteronomy 4:2 says, you shall not add to the word which I command you, neither shall you diminish it, that you may keep the commandments of the Lord your God which I command you. Verse 12:32 says, whatever I command you, be watchful to do it; you shall not add to it or diminish it. Here comes the curse in Galatians 1:9, as we said before, so I now say again: If anyone is preaching to you a gospel different from or contrary to that which you received [from us], let him be accursed. All biblical curses are centered on deviant from the standard of God.

Satanic blessing is a curse.

There might be someone in your life, society or you must have heard of such a now-deceased grandfather, father, mother, uncle or friend who belonged to an occult society, supposed he/she was bringing blessing, progress or to reverse a lingered financial incapacitation upon his descendants but because he was seeking the supernatural outside of Jesus, his attempted blessing was actually inviting evil spirits to intervene and dwell in the lives of his descendants.

Though progress might seem positively effective at the beginning but the end thereof brings restlessness, weeping, conflicts or even sequential of death. I have seen a case where someone sacrificed his children to oracles just to maintain an incessant flow of money, good luck or even to live longer. Some impatient Christians had sought for the fruit of the womb through the spiritual means, the spiritist will definitely grant you children but these children will be a thorn on your flesh, source of sorrow and parasitic. Most of children gotten from satanic means are either perpetual handicaps or incurable nuisance to the family and society.

Mere informing these spirits that the unpleasant effects of their actions are unwanted would change nothing. That would be like continuing to get drunk while telling the bartender you no longer want hangovers. Every one involved in such occult practices regrets at last because Satan gives nothing free, he maneuvers to destroy the souls of men. He so much enjoys setting our lives on fire. The book of Proverbs chapter 10 verses 22 clearly states, The blessing of the LORD makes a person rich, and he adds no sorrow with it." Moreover, the only way to get rid of these curses is to submit totally to the Lordship of Christ Jesus.

God does not delight in the suffering of His people, He wish above all things that we should flourish like a tree by the riverside but being that He does not conform with iniquities, our sin often separates us from His divine coverage. When we are not under His divine coverage, Satan can do abundantly all he wishes to us, which in effect could be immediate or later. Sin activates curses, giving demons a legal ground in ones life.

According to Christian dogma, all humanity is thus cursed with original sin. Jesus, in turn, takes this curse on himself in order to redeem humanity. This freedom is actively manifested in the life of only those who faithfully believe in Christ Jesus as it is written; whosoever believes in Him shall be saved. The following verses conforms our deliverance but only when we totally submit to God in every area of our life.

God hath delivered us from the power of darkness, and hath translated us into the kingdom of his dear Son. Colossians 1:13. Christ hath redeemed us from the curse of the law, being made a curse for us: for it is written, Cursed is every one that hangeth on a tree. Galatians 3:13 But the Lord is faithful, who shall establish you, and keep you from evil. 2 Thessalonians 3:3.Who gave himself for us, that he might redeem us from all iniquity, and purify unto himself a peculiar people, zealous of good works.

Titus 2:14, Eph 3:20: Now unto him that is able to do exceeding abundantly above all that we ask or think, according to the power that worketh in us. Gal 3:27 for as many of you as have been baptized into Christ have put on Christ. Phil 4:7: and the peace of God, which passeth all understanding, shall keep your hearts and minds through Christ Jesus. Gal 3:26 for ye are all the children of God by faith in Christ Jesus. Hebrews 10:14 for by one offering he hath perfected for ever them that are sanctified. Hebrews 13:6 So that we may boldly say, the Lord is my helper, and I will not fear what man shall do unto me.

Where Jesus lives, there are no more curses:

Revelation 22:3 and there shall be no more curses: but the throne of God and of the Lamb shall be in it; and his servants shall serve him: Colossians 2:10 and ye are complete in him, which is the head of all principality and power. 2 Tim 1:7 For God hath not given us the spirit of fear; but of power, and of love, and of a sound mind. However, when we compromise the word of God, when we deviate from God's standard, curse can actively work in our lives.

UNPROFITABLE COVENANT

Covenant/Soul ties simply mean uniting together in one mind and focus. It could also be referred to as treaties, alliances, agreements, compacts, pledges, mutual agreements, promises, and undertakings for or on behalf of another. A soul tie can serve many functions, but in its simplest form, it ties two souls together in the spiritual realm. Vows are known to bind the soul (Numbers 30:2), just as marriage vows that binds the two people together (Ephesians 5:31).

Soul ties could be agreements between two equals as in

Abraham with Abimelech (Gen. 21:25-33),

Joshua with the People at Shechem (Joshua 24:19-27),

David and Jonathan (1 Sam. 23:15-18),

Jacob and Laban (Genesis 31-44-54),

Solomon and Shimei (1 Kings 2:36-46),

Asa and Benhadad: (1 Kings 15:17-22)

It can also stand between a king or leader and his subjects, God and individuals or God and nations, as in:

God and Abraham {Genesis 15:17-21}, God and Noah {Genesis 9:11-17}.

Soul ties with God as in Deuteronomy 10:20 states, "You shall fear the Lord your God; you shall serve Him and cling to Him, and by His name and presence you shall swear." Cling or cleave means to cling or adhere, cleave (fast together) or be joined together.

Having a soul tie with the Lord is very important for our daily Christian living. We must be committed to the Lord and His service, as Jesus said, "...I and My Father are one..."

Soul ties with fellow Christians is also evident in Ephesians 4:16 "For because of Him the whole body (the church, in all its various parts), closely joined and firmly knit together by the joints and ligaments with which it is supplied, when each part [with power adapted to its need] is working properly [in all its functions], grows to full maturity, building itself up in love."

Colossians 2:2 "[For my concern is] that their hearts may be braced (comforted, cheered, and encouraged) as they are knit together..." v 19) "and not holding fast to the Head, from Whom the entire body, supplied and knit together by means of its joints and ligaments, grows with a growth that is from God." Godly soul ties within believers are normal, because believers are required to love and help each other; as it is written "Love thy neighbor as thyself." We are one body Christ Jesus.

There are also Soul ties within friends, See - I Samuel 18:1 "When David had finished speaking to Saul, the soul of Jonathan was knit with the soul of David, and Jonathan loved him as his own life." Soul ties within pastors or leaders; see - II Samuel 20:2 "So all the men of Israel withdrew from David and followed Sheba son of Bicri: but the men of Judah stayed faithfully with their king, from the Jordan to Jerusalem." Soul ties with your husband/wife - Genesis 2:24 "Therefore a man shall leave his father and his mother and shall become united and cleave to his wife, and they shall become one flesh."

Unprofitable covenant or what can be called unholy covenant {soul ties with the world} is the creation of an unholy agreement between two equal or unequal beings. In the secular world, an in-depth sight into man and woman relationship has shown that unfaithfulness hurts when you really love someone, so what they thought best to avoid ending up with a high blood pressure is to give the person the benefit of doubt by making him or her to take an oath that he/she would not cheat or jilt on you in the near future. Unholy alliances of any type will not only put us outside the will of God but prevents our life from being blessed.

Similarly, some evil societies especially the occult group will mandate their members to make an oath of faithfulness and sincerity, to keep secret of all the atrocities and devilish commitment. Sometimes, the quest for solution to a particular problem has lured many Christians into demonic covenants unknowingly as for those that seek the fruit of womb outside Christ Jesus. We are bond with Satan whenever we sin

The book of Proverbs 6:2 said, "Thou art snared with the words of thy mouth, thou art taken with the words of thy mouth." These spoken covenants need to be renounced in order to break the soul tie because when you renounce something, you basically have taken them back verbally. For example, if a woman has had a soul tie with a man who was not the one, and said she would never be able to love another man, then this needs to be renounced if she wants to break the soul tie. Such a woman could renounce it by saying something like, "I renounce having said that I will never be able to love another man." Verbally renouncing something carries a lot of weight in the spiritual realm. Just as vows can bind the soul, renouncing can release the soul from bondage.

IDOLATRY

Idolatry can be defined as "worship or reverence given to any created object or person." It actually takes many forms, not just the "praying to statues" that many people think of when they hear the word "idolatry." Rather it is biblically understood as the tendency to value something or someone in a way that it hinders the love and trust we owe to God; the substitution of the likeness of an image of corruptible man, of birds, of animals, of reptiles and of material possessions for the glory of the incorruptible God.

It also could be attaching more importance to the gift and not the giver. Idolatry conflicts with our putting God alone first in our lives, in what we love and trust (see Exodus 20:3-5; Deut. 5:7-9; Romans 1:21-23). Idolatry is making something or someone that to which we look up to bring happiness, peace, fulfillment, contentment, and all the things only God is supposed to provide us, which in essence is the definition of a false god. To put it another way, idolatry is fashioning and forming false gods, or idols, out of one's own vain imaginations.

This practice is mostly centered on the mind and one of the fundamental elements of evil comprising the carnal nature, or sin nature, which actually is the nature of the devil himself, and which is also alluded to as the "spirit of disobedience as seen in Ephesians 2 vs.2. Most Christians including the so-called anointed Ministers attached more values on material things than kingdom issues. We have created new forms of false gods like money, power over others, materialism, even relationship and sports have become our false god. When we become consumed by our desire, we are prone to turning away from God, His command to Love Him, and loving our neighbor as our self.

Considering the questions below will give us a clearer understanding about idolatry; Is it idolatry to say that we cannot be saved unless Mary helps us? That would mean that the sacrifice of Jesus Christ was not sufficient to save us. Some Popes have declared that there is no salvation apart from Mary. Is it idolatry to say that there is no salvation without the Pope? Again, that would mean that Jesus is not enough. Some popes have declared that no person can be saved unless he or she submits to the Pope. Is it idolatry to call the Pope "Holy Father"? In the Bible, that term is only used for God.

Jesus used it when praying to His heavenly Father. (John 17:11) Is it idolatry to sing hymns to the Pope? It is traditional to sing papal hymns. Is it idolatry to say that the Pope is less than God but more than man; who shall judge all and be judged by no one? Does it promote idolatry when a Pope declares, we hold upon this earth the place of God Almighty? Is it idolatry to address the Pope as Your Holiness? The protocol of the Catholic Church requires it.

Is it idolatry to venerate Mary and the saints? According to "Webster's Dictionary," one definition of "veneration" is "expressing reverent feeling; worship" and one definition of "devotion" is "religious fervor". Catholic Canon Law says that all Catholics should cultivate devotion to Mary, including praying the rosary. The rosary has ten prayers to Mary for every one prayer to God. Every fixed altar in churches is required to have a relic of a saint. Is it idolatry to venerate "images"? Canon Law says that Catholic churches should have "holy images" (statues, pictures, etc.) and that Catholics should venerate these images.

In contrast, the Bible forbids the veneration of statues or other images. It says, "Thou shall not make thee any graven image, or any likeness of any thing that is in heaven above, or that is in the earth beneath, or that is in the waters beneath the earth: Thou shall not bow down thyself unto them, nor serve them" (Deuteronomy 5:8-9). The Infant of Prague is an example of the extent to which veneration of images can be taken. It is a statue of Jesus as a baby kept in a church in Prague, Czechoslovakia. Miracles are attributed to this statue. Pilgrims come from around the world to venerate it. The statue wears expensive clothing and a gold crown set with jewels. It has 70 different sets of clothes.

In 1995 it was carried in solemn procession through the streets of Prague. The procession was led by two cardinals. Churches in many countries have replicas of this statue. Is it idolatry to worship consecrated bread? The Catholic Church says that during Mass the bread and wine literally turn into the body, blood, soul and divinity of Jesus Christ. Catholics are taught to bow before the bread and to worship it. According to Catholic Canon Law, Catholics are supposed to worship the Eucharist with "supreme adoration". If the answer to any of these questions is "yes," then the Catholic Church teaches its members to practice idolatry.

Other forms of false worship are astrology, Satanism, witchcraft, and any ideology which undermine our faith and cause us to turn away from God our Creator. *Their idols are silver and gold, the work of men's hands. They have mouths, but they speak not; eyes have they, but they see not .They that make them are like unto them; so is everyone that trusted in them declares Psalm 115.* God is not a respecter of any person and frowns seriously at any man, kindred or generation that denies Him the due glory.

He directly imposes a consequence that only repentance can alleviate as seen in Romans 1 vs.25 to 32 "because of their idolatry, God gave them over to shameful lusts. Even their women exchanged natural relations for unnatural ones. In the same way, the men also abandoned natural relations with women and were inflamed with lust for one another. Men committed indecent acts with other men, and received in themselves the due penalty for their perversion.

Furthermore, since they did not think it worthwhile to retain the knowledge of God, He gave them over to a depraved mind; to do what ought not to be done. They have become filled with every kind of wickedness, evil, greed, depravity, envy, murder, strife, deceit and malice. They are gossips, slanderers, God-haters, insolent, arrogant and boastful; they invent ways of doing evil; they disobey their parents; they are senseless, faithless, heartless, and ruthless. Although they know God's righteous decree that those who do such things deserve death, they not only continue to do these very things but also approve of those who practice them. Idolatry alienates us from God, His protection and love.

~ 10 ~

Familiar Spirits and Familiar Items

The word "familiar" in this usage is derived from the Latin word "familiaris", meaning a "household servant," which means some spirits are made man-servant. A familiar spirit is a demon that obeys, serves, prompts or helps a witch, conjurer, or other users of the supernatural. The Bible clearly recorded that all sorcerers, necromancer or anyone who claimed the ability to contact the dead have this familiar spirit. Deut.18:11; 2 Kings 21:6; 2 Chronicle 33:6; Lev.19:31; 20:6; Isa 8:19; 29:4.

It is the designation of a specific type of evil spirit, so classified because of its chief characteristic, "familiarity" and "relationship" with a person or personality. A familiar spirit is a demon whom a Satanist has developed close communication with, and is used basically for spying and information gathering purposes. One of the greatest dangers of familiar spirits is they appear just the same as the gift of the Holy Spirit. It could be any of the gifts: the word of wisdom or the word of knowledge, faith or the gift of healings, working of miracles or prophecy, discerning of spirits or different kinds of tongues, even the interpretation of tongues. Familiar spirits counterfeits the work of the Holy Spirit.

They do look and seem real to the natural eye. Consider the story we find in the book of Acts 16:16-18, in Macedonia, where the slave girl with the spirit of divination (prophesy) followed Paul and those with him around saying: "These men are the servants of the most High God who proclaim to us the way of salvation."To the natural ear this woman would have seemed to be holy and uplifting but what she was really being was a disruption and hindrance. However, through the gift of discernment, Paul knew exactly what was working through her. Paul, under the anointing of the Holy Spirit, commanded that evil spirit to come out of her and within the same hour she was delivered of that familiar spirit.

In spirit filled churches the most prominent familiar spirit found is either the spirit of prophesy or the gift of tongues although all may be present and any of them can be working. We cannot detect a familiar spirit with ordinary eyes. Only a person operating in the gift of discernment can detect these evil entities in operation. Pray continuously for the gift of discernment and you will never be led astray by a lying spirit. When a demon is placed within an animal by a witch and the witch can then through her communication with the demon both control the animal, see and hear everything the animal sees and hears.

A witch can also astral project her own human spirit into an animal and then control the animal for her own use. In our time, the enchanter, charmer, consulter, wizard, necromancer, herbalist, white garment churches, clairvoyants, hypnotist, palm readers, tarot card readers, voodoo experts and many others are examples of Satanist that uses familiar spirits to influence people with lies and deceit. Any involvement with familiar spirits constitutes idolatry and creates spiritual defilement thus the Bible warns us to "regard not them that have familiar spirits neither seek after wizards to be defiled by them, I am the Lord your God " Lev 19:31 "There shall not be found among you anyone that maketh his son or daughter to pass through fire or that useth divination or observer of times or an enchanter or witch or a charmer or a consulter or a necromancer" Deut 18:10-11.

Familiar spirit can gain entrance into a person's life through divination, transcendental meditation, visualization, necromancer, witchcraft, drugs and alcohol. These spirits {demons} respond quickly to the summons of the medium, example of this medium is seen in the book of 1 Sam 28:7 where Saul consulted the witch of Endor. They are go-between, which forms a communication link between the earthly world and the demonic realm.

When a person forms a relationship with an evil spirit, which could be done either willfully or ignorantly he then has a familiar spirit. In the book of Leviticus 19:31; 20:6; 20:27 and Deuteronomy 18:9-14 they were referred to as "mediums and familiar spirits and forbids being involved in them...because they are an abomination to the Lord. Sometimes rejection, inferiority, insecurity and hopeless situations will often prone Christians to crave intimacy with the Lord through the unbiblical ways of getting closer to Him. When good things are sought the wrong ways, the devil takes immediate advantage of us.

There are many avenues through which familiar spirits can be acquired.

(i) **Divination**: this is an attempt to discern future events or to discover that which cannot be known by normal methods as Saul did. "There shall not be found among you anyone that useth divination...Deut 18:9-10."You shall not ....practice divination or soothsaying.Lev 19:26.

(ii) **Transcendental Meditation**: this practice is widely practiced by Hindu worshippers and is been taught in schools all through western countries. In an attempt to discover true enlightenment, self-identity and willpower they mind is being open to deceiving spirits who impersonate deity and divulge false revelation of secret and hidden mysteries.

(iii) Having invisible companion and playmates.

(iv). **Visualization**: visualization is not a valid spiritual tool, although it is a common technique employed by some practitioner of inner healing and healing of the memories.

(v) **Drugs:** hallucinatory drugs provide channels into the demonic realm. These drugs alter the function of the brain cells, pacing way for an infinite variety of supposed revelations which are fostered by familiar spirits that were contacted via the drug induced hallucination.

(vi). **Conversing with demons during deliverance**. During deliverance, the challenged demons sometimes speak through the indwelled person. Through these interrogations the deliverance worker may develop a relationship with these demons.

Conversing with demons can easily lead to the forbidden role of being a "consulter with familiar spirits".

If one becomes a communication link with the demonic realm, he becomes a spiritist medium and the information he transmits is a doctrine that demons teach. Therefore, Christians ought to be filled with the Holy Spirit, with love, with joy, and with the fullness of life that comes from Jesus Christ. We are also to be on guard, "for our struggle is not against flesh and blood, but against the rulers, against the authorities, against the powers of this dark world and against the spiritual forces of evil in the heavenly realms"

Familiar Items

These are items to which demons are infested or clung. Anything used in worshipping Satan is a legal ground for demons. These familiar spirits- witches, psychics, and Satan worshiper- uses playing cards, burning of incense, burning of candles for divination and to cast spells and curses. Some objects, particularly rings, bracelets, necklaces and other jewelry as a gift from a witch or the like may have curses or demons clung in them.

In antique shops there are often selections of rings, pendants, pins and various kinds of jewelry which were originally designed to bring good luck and to act as a talisman to chase evil. Common familiar objects are object of occulted arts, any rock and roll music, tapes, posters, T-shirts, mermaid artificial hairs, materials for manicure and pedicure, role-playing fantasy games, any artifacts of eastern and Asian religions such as statues of gods {buhhda }as souvenirs, any rosaries or object used in the practice of Catholicism, articles of masonry practices, any pagan religion, necklaces with crucifix also clairvoyance, hypnotist, palm reading, tarot card reading, voodoo experts are all demon infested.

Also a Satanist can invoke demons into a specific non-occult object like gifts and presents. Most of the latest productions, advancement in technologies, fashions, and latest cars are indirect inspirational work of demons. The purpose which is to impose direct demonic channels and influence in the life and family of the user, thereby causing disorder, confusion and illness.

Also, the Egyptian ankh (a cross with a loop at the top which was an ancient fertility symbol); the ancient witchcraft sign of the broken cross, popularly know as the peace symbol; Chais (consists of Hebrew characters spelling the word life); all kinds of Polynesian tikkis, figures, and other things; a wiggly tail which is called the "Italian horn"; protectors from the evil eye; a hand with the index and little fingers pointing up (a satanic witchcraft sign); and a great variety of crosses, clovers, stars, wishbones, lucky coins, mystic medals, horseshoes, statues of gods, statues of cats and other items.

The graven images of their gods shall you burn with fire: thou shall not desire they silver or gold that is in them, nor take it unto thee lest thou be snared therein: for it is an abomination to the Lord thy God. Neither shall thou be cursed thou be cursed thing like it; but thou shall utterly detest it and thou shall utterly abhor kit, for it is a cursed thing". God's warnings over the used of these accursed things are highlighted in the scriptures. 1 Corinthians 10:19-20; Deut 7:25-26.

In a typical African society, when a child is serious ill, certain objects are tired round his/her waist, neck or hands with believe to scare away evil-spirits of sickness but reverse is normally the case. Peoples' bodies could be pierced and inserted with either bone particles or talisman in the name of traditional marks. These are links to demonic influence in the lives of many.

The use of these items denies us God's presence and protection as seen in the account of Achan who brought in defiled things into the tabernacle caused Israel to fell before their enemies. I will not be with you anymore unless you destroy whatever among you is devoted to destruction. Joshua 7.

Hypnosis is another big doorway for demons to have a legal ground in ones life. The person being hypnotized must subject his will to the hypnotist, open to anything the hypnotist chooses to put into him. Hypnosis is a mental state of heightened suggestibility characterized by trance-like sleep. The basis thereof is the fixation of the subject's attention upon a gradually narrowing source of stimulation until he is attendant upon only the direction of the hypnotist.

A researcher said" hypnotic induction consists of a system of verbal and nonverbal manipulation to lead a person into a heightened state of suggestibility more simply a condition in which one will believe almost anything...graft onto their memories, fantasies or suggestion deliberately or unwittingly communicated by the hypnotist and that after hypnosis the subject cannot differentiate between a true recollection and a fantasy or suggested detail. Hypnosis to stop smoking or control eating to lose weight is demonic healing so is any practice of Transcendental meditation or yoga brings demonic bondage.

A hypnotized mind will automatically believe anything, loses its ability to differentiate truth from false thereby making easier to be deceived. Deut 18:10-12. There are difference between Godly meditation and satanic meditation. The latter involves the blanking out of the mind and clearing it of all thoughts thereby making it empty and free: phrases, quotations or recitations are been repeated over and over. Cosmic feelings brings demon to settle in ones life.

~ 11 ~

<u>Our Victory</u>

The hope and desire of every born again Christian is to live a spiritually and physically fruitful life but having known that our enemy is warring tirelessly to hinder our eternal expectations, we must stand and resist him. For though we walk in the flesh, we do not war after the flesh: for the weapons of our warfare are not carnal, but mighty through God to the pulling down of strongholds 2 Corinthians 10:3-4. The book of Matthew 4 verses 1 to 11 and Luke 4 verses 1 to 13 recorded the grand climax to a sinless life during which Jesus triumphed over the enemy repeatedly.

Here again, Satan probably rejoiced in the death of Christ, believing this to be a victory for him, but like all his victories, this one, too, was short-lived. The death of Christ on the cross is the basis for Satan's final defeat and when Jesus rose from the grave, Satan was finally defeated (Hebrew 2:14-15; 1 Peter 3:18, 22). Having been thus raised from among the dead, Christ Jesus was exalted by God to His own right hand in the heavenlies. Though resurrection had been opposed by the tremendous "powers o f the air":-"all principality, and power, and might, and dominion, and every name that is name.

They had, however, been baffled and overthrown and the risen Lord had been enthroned "far above" them, ruling with the authority of the Most High. This is the foundation of our victory over Satan. The devil is defeated as far as the believer is concerned. Therefore it is important that a believer recognizes the power and authority delegated to him through Christ Jesus. Christ Jesus has reclaimed the lost dominion and control for us. All we need to do is to submit ourselves to God, resist the devil and he will flee from us. We must accept total mastership of Jesus in every area of our life.

Jesus has given this authority to us, His followers. **Luke 9:1, 2** says, and then he called his twelve disciples together, and gave them power and **authority** over all devils, and to cure diseases. And he sent them to preach the kingdom of God, and to heal the sick. **Mark 13:34** tells us, for the Son of man is as a man taking a far journey, who left his house, and gave authority to his servants, and to every man his work, and commanded the porter to watch. And he said unto them, Go ye into all the world, and preach the gospel to every creature. ... And these signs shall follow them that believe; In my name shall they cast out devils; they shall speak with new tongues; they shall take up serpents; and if they drink any deadly thing, it shall not hurt them; they shall lay hands on the sick, and they shall recover. **Mark 16:15, 17, 18**.

You might say, "Wait a minute. If Satan is defeated, then why does he seem to be defeating me?" It is worthy of note that for a Christian to live a spiritually fulfilled life, he must examine every facet of his life to see if there are doorways or loopholes that gives Satan and demons a chance in his life. Remember that Satan baits his hook with the desires of our flesh, mind eyes and pride of life {1 John 2:16}. The person caught by Satan thinks he is doing his own will when in reality the devil is manipulating him.

For us to exercise this delegated authority over Satan and other evil circumstances of life, we must abstain from sin. It is obvious that sins especially sexual sins opens wide the doorways for demons to attack our life. Sin in its nature is failure, error, and transgression, unrighteousness in thought, action or speech.

Sin makes us miss the mark of Divine Standard. How will God spare or protect us if God did not spare angels when they sinned, but sent them to hell, putting them into gloomy dungeons to be held for judgment. The books of 2 Peter 2:4, Matthew 27:4 and Luke 15:18, 21 clearly illustrated how sin can rob us of our divine standards. Sin insubordinates God's authority and His delegated power on us.

Sin is lawlessness. Sin is breaking divine law because the carnal mind is enmity against God: for it is not subject to the law of God, neither indeed can be. Romans 8:7. We should have confidence in God. Trusting in God, acknowledgement of our helplessness, sinfulness, and lost condition makes us freed from Satan's power. We should accept the gift of salvation as offered to us in Christ and stand before God clothed in His son's righteousness. Phil 3:9; Titus 3:5 Importantly, failure in one's duty and financial indebtedness are sins that seem so insignificant in the life of a Christian. We should not avoid paying our tithe. *You are under a curse ...because you are robbing me.... Mal 3:10.*

Every tithe due for God should be paid, as this is God's command. Tithe evasion attracts the curse of God on us. When we are under the curse of God, His protection and provision are not for us. Financial debt can and always contributes to spiritual failure. Financial worries constitute a portion of the "cares of this life" that result in not bearing fruit to God's glory. The book of Luke 8:14 illustrate to us about the seed that fell among thorns and were choked with the worries of life.

Also marriage failure, mental depravity, and emotional problems are all often connected to financial indebtedness. Families are deteriorating often because both the mother and father are so deeply in debt that they are working long hours just to try to keep from going under or experiencing bankruptcy. In many cases, by being diligent and industrious in labor we can avoid objectionable debt. The Christian is to be the opposite of sloth and laziness

(Col. 3: 22, 23). The teaching of the wise man is always applicable: "Whatsoever thy hand fined to do, do it with thy might..." (Eccl. 9: 10, contrast with Prov. 6: 6-11). Debt is a sin as deduced from verses below: Matthew 6:12; Matthew 18:32; Romans 1:14; also Luke 7:41.When we flee from sin, devil will have no legal ground to torment us. All we simply need to do is to remind him of whom he is "a defeated foe".

We cannot freely exercise our authority over Satan when are having things that belongs to him. We cannot cast out demons and embrace devil, rebuking Satan while we are comfortably enjoying his food is the greatest mistake of our time. Obviously, we have forgotten that his food nourishes nothing but shame, guilt, destruction and death. Total abstinence from the use of any demonic inclined objects like occult books, Ouija boards, Tarots card, crystal balls, palm reading, fortunetellers, horoscopes, astrology, clairvoyance, fantasy games, hypnotism, and trance channeling is imperative to blockade Satan from our life.

A mere unconscious participation in these acts gives Satan and his demons legal ground to attack us. The word is clear about this *"Now the works of the flesh are evident: sexual immorality, impurity, sensuality, idolatry, sorcery, enmity, strife, jealousy, fits of anger, rivalries, dissensions, divisions, envy, drunkenness, orgies, and things like these. I warn you, as I warned you before, that those who do such things will not inherit the kingdom of God Gal.5:19-21. Beloved, do not imitate evil but imitate good. Whoever does good is from God; whoever does evil has not seen God 3 John 1:11. Abstain from all appearance of evil. And the very God of peace sanctify you wholly; and I pray God your whole spirit and soul and body be preserved blameless unto the coming of our Lord Jesus Christ. 1 Thess.5:22, 23.*

Finally, using the metaphorical example of an equipped Roman Army as used by Paul, we should prepare for warfare with Satan with the spiritual armor as clearly stated in Ephesians 6:10-18

[i] **The belt of Truth**: to put on the belt of truth is to put on the Lord Jesus Christ. Christ is the way, the truth and the life. Romans 14:6. Since Satan depends on deceit to maintain his power, our defense should be the truth. We should not distort or closed the truth regardless any advantage it could pose to us. Devil is a liar, John 8:44, when our life is controlled by the truth, Christ Jesus will defeat him.

[ii] **The Breastplate of Righteousness**: The metallic breastplate worn by the ancient Romans soldier covers their body from the neck to the waist both front and back. This represents our righteousness in Christ and righteous life in Christ.2 Corinthians 5:21; Ephesians 4:24. Any sin in our life leaves us open to Satan's attacks. Even though we are given the righteousness of Christ, [2 Corinthians 5:21]. We must continually put on the protection of holy living. Therefore, when Satan accuses us, we can count on God's righteousness to protect our hearts. Revelation 12:10.

[iii] **The shoes of the gospel of peace**. We should be at peace with God. Romans 5:1 and at peace with man to defeat the Devil. Hebrew 12:14; James 4:1-7.We must be prepared to share the gospel of peace with sinners. When our feet are planted on the truth, we are at peace with God and He is on our side, then we can stand firmly against Satan's attacks.

[iv] .**The shield of faith**: the shield protects the soldier from spears, arrows and fiery darts of the enemy. Satan shoots fiery darts at our heart and minds, lie, blasphemous thought, doubt, sinful desires and more are his fiery darts. In order to quench these fiery darts, we must trust and believe what God has said about every area of our life.

[v] **The helmet of salvation or deliverance**: Satan delights so much in attacking our mind as he keeps flashing thoughts of fear, doubt and discouragement. Our fears exist in the mind, but God will deliver us from Satan's arrows of fear, anxieties and devilish

conception. John 10:28-29; Heb 7:25 and 1 Peter 1:5.The helmet of salvation is our hope of eternal glory. It protects us against Satan's two-edged sword.

[vi] **The sword of the Spirit**: the word of God is the basis of our faith. We should learn and yield its authority. The scripture is our best offensive and defensive weapon against the devil. We should memorize the scripture, as many verses as possible because an out loudly recitation of it sets the devil on the run. These verses should be recited whenever we are in trouble.

[vii] Through constant prayer, expressing our dependence on God, we can defeat the foe. The strength of the Lord and the power of his might is ours. Ephesians 6:10. Thanksgiving is also a great prayer weapon for defeating Satan. We should also intercede for others as this can bring victory to our own lives.

[viii] **We should not under estimate Satan's power**. We must always be conscious of his ceaseless attacks on us... Be sober, be vigilant because your adversary the devil as a roaring lion walketh about seeking whom he may devour 2 Peter 5:8.

[ix] **We must learn to hear the Lord speak to us**. Certain conditions are critical, complicated and complex. We should refrain from human ideology in situations like this. The Holy Spirit will put thoughts into our mind. The spirit itself beareth witness with our spirit that we are the children of God Romans 8:16

Wherefore as the Holy Ghost saith, today if ye will hear his voice, harden not your hearts as in the provocation, in the day of temptation in the wilderness. The Lord shall deliver you from every evil work, and will preserve you unto his heavenly kingdom, to him be glory forever and ever Amen. God bless you.